## Introduction to *The Interview Blueprint: Build Confidence and Win Any Job*

In today's competitive job market, the ability to interview well is a skill as valuable as any technical qualification. No matter how impressive your resume or how vast your experience, the interview is where employers ultimately decide whether you're the right fit for the role. It's the moment where you translate your qualifications into a compelling story and showcase the confidence and competence that will make you stand out from the crowd.

But let's face it: interviews can be daunting. Whether you're preparing for your first interview or stepping into a high stakes executive role, it's normal to feel pressure. Interviewing is a skill that combines research, communication, self-awareness, and adaptability. Many talented professionals struggle not because they lack the ability, but because they don't know how to present themselves effectively. This is where *The Interview Blueprint* comes in.

This book offers a step-by-step guide to mastering the interview process, from preparation to follow-up. It's designed to build your confidence and provide a structured approach to navigating common questions, addressing potential challenges, and creating lasting impressions. Each chapter breaks down critical elements of interviewing: understanding the company, crafting your personal brand, communicating your value proposition, and managing tricky questions with ease. You'll learn how to turn nerves into focus, articulate your strengths, and approach interviews as an opportunity to shine rather than an ordeal to survive.

*The Interview Blueprint* isn't just about answering questions it's about learning how to tell your story in a way that resonates with employers. By the end of this book, you'll have the tools to present your best self in any interview, from entry level positions to senior management roles, and across industries from healthcare to tech. You'll know how to leave a lasting impression, how to ask insightful questions, and how to take control of your interview process with confidence.

Whether you've faced rejections, feel unsure about your interview skills, or just want to polish your approach, this book will serve as your guide. Packed with practical advice, examples, and actionable strategies, *The Interview Blueprint* will transform how you approach interviews and ultimately, how you advance your career.

It's time to go beyond preparation and build the confidence that wins jobs. Let's get started.

## About the Author: Seán O'Connor – Interview Coaching Expert

Seán O'Connor is a highly respected interview coach, author, and healthcare professional with over 30 years of experience across diverse industries. Throughout his career, Seán has developed a unique understanding of human behaviour, communication, and the skills necessary to navigate high-stakes situations like job interviews.

Known for his tailored, results driven coaching style, Seán has helped countless individuals from entry-level candidates to senior executives succeed in interviews by improving their communication and presentation skills. His coaching focuses on building confidence, personal branding, and developing effective strategies for handling even the toughest interview questions. Seán's ability to break down the interview process into manageable steps allows his clients to approach each opportunity with clarity and purpose.

As the founder of Seán O'Connor Coaching, he delivers one-on-one coaching sessions, seminars, and workshops designed to empower job seekers and professionals looking to advance their careers. His hands on approach teaches individuals how to articulate their value, use the STAR method for answering behavioural questions, and ask insightful questions that leave a strong impression on interviewers.

In addition to his interview coaching, Seán has extensive experience working within the Health Service Executive (HSE) in Ireland, managing key programme. His leadership roles have included Director of the Dyslexia Association of Ireland and Chairperson of Pieta House, adding depth to his expertise in understanding diverse needs and perspectives in professional settings.

Drawing from his background in counselling, criminal justice, and project management, Seán understands the critical role that communication plays in career advancement. His work across multiple sectors, including healthcare, education, and addiction services, has reinforced his belief in the power of strategic communication particularly in interview settings.

Seán is also the author of 30 books, including guides on mental health and well-being, and his newest project focuses on sharing his deep knowledge of interview skills with a broader audience. His proven methods have already transformed the careers of many, and in this book, Seán provides readers with the tools they need to ace any interview and land their dream job.

All of Seán's publications can be found at

https://www.amazon.co.uk/~/e/B0C8G4ZN94

**Where you can contact him**

Seán O'Connor Coaching

https://www.seanoconnorcoaching.com/

Contents

**Introduction: The Power of a Great Interview – Page 8**

- Importance of interview skills
- Common challenges and misconceptions
- How interviews have evolved in today's job market

**Chapter 1: Preparing Like a Pro – Page 23**

- Researching the company and role
- Understanding job descriptions and tailoring responses
- Practising common interview questions
- Importance of personal branding and your value proposition

**Chapter 2: Building Confidence – Page 50**

- Mindset techniques to reduce anxiety
- Body language: non-verbal cues to look confident
- How to develop a confident communication style

**Chapter 3: The First Impression – Page 70**

- Crafting the perfect introduction: the "elevator pitch"
- How to dress for success
- Creating rapport with interviewers

## Chapter 4: Handling Common Interview Questions – Page 89

- STAR method for behavioural questions
- How to discuss weaknesses effectively
- Answering salary expectation questions tactfully

## Chapter 5: Asking the Right Questions – Page 105

- Why you should ask questions as an interviewee
- Examples of insightful questions to ask about the role, company culture, and team dynamics
- What questions to avoid

## Chapter 6: Navigating Tricky Situations – Page 120

- Dealing with stress and unexpected questions
- Handling panel interviews and video interviews
- Strategies for overcoming a poor start

## Chapter 7: Following Up and Negotiating Offers – Page 135

- Crafting a standout thank-you note
- Managing multiple job offers or delays in response
- How to negotiate salary and benefits effectively

## Chapter 8: Interview Skills for Different Contexts – Page 151

- Tailoring your approach for internal promotions, entry-level positions, and senior roles
- Industry-specific interview tips (e.g., healthcare, tech, arts, etc.)
- How to handle interviews for freelance or contract work

**Conclusion: Becoming an Interview Master – Page 169**

- Continuous improvement: learning from feedback and failed interviews
- How to stay prepared for future opportunities

**Appendices – Page 179**

- Sample interview questions and answers
- Interview checklists
- Useful resources for further learning (books, websites, etc.)

## Introduction: The Power of a Great Interview

Interviews are not just about answering questions; they are the most crucial stage in the hiring process where you, as a candidate, have the opportunity to make a lasting impression on potential employers. The ability to handle an interview well is often the deciding factor between landing a job and being passed over for another candidate. A great interview doesn't just showcase your skills and qualifications; it is a conversation where you demonstrate your suitability for a role and your alignment with the company's values and goals. This is why mastering interview skills is essential for career success, regardless of industry or experience level.

## The Importance of Interview Skills

Interview skills are the toolkit that allows candidates to turn potential into reality. Being well qualified on paper is essential, but your ability to articulate those qualifications in a personal and compelling way is often what makes the difference. Here are some of the key reasons why developing strong interview skills is critical:

### 1. First Impressions Matter:

An interview is usually your first face-to-face or virtual interaction with a prospective employer. Studies show that first impressions are formed within the first 7 seconds of meeting someone. During an interview, these impressions are shaped by everything from your appearance and body language to the way you greet the interviewer and introduce yourself. A well prepared candidate understands how to project confidence, professionalism, and interest in the role right from the start.

*Example*: Imagine two candidates with equal qualifications. One arrives looking disorganised, fumbles through their introduction, and answers questions hesitantly. The other presents a strong handshake, maintains eye contact, and delivers a clear, concise summary of their experience. Even if their CVs are identical, the second candidate will leave a far better impression simply due to their ability to communicate effectively.

**2. Showcasing More Than Your CV:**

A CV or résumé provides an overview of your skills, but an interview gives you the chance to provide context, demonstrate personality, and show your interpersonal skills. Employers are not just looking for someone who can perform the tasks required; they want someone who fits into the team and company culture. Interview skills enable you to communicate your soft skills, such as emotional intelligence, adaptability, and problem-solving abilities, which are harder to convey in writing.

*Example*: During the interview, you can narrate a story about how you handled a challenging project or navigated a complex team dynamic, giving the employer a real sense of your approach to problem solving and collaboration.

**3. Confidence and Competence Are Linked:**

Great interview skills help bridge the gap between confidence and competence. Even if you are highly skilled, the inability to convey that clearly in an interview may leave the employer uncertain about your potential. Being able to speak fluently about your experiences, qualifications, and aspirations allows you to position yourself as the best candidate for the job. Effective interview preparation also helps you anticipate difficult questions, ensuring you're not caught off-guard, which can boost your confidence during the conversation.

*Example*: If asked about a gap in your employment, a well-prepared candidate won't stumble or become defensive but will instead explain how they used that time productively, such as upskilling or reflecting on their career direction, turning what could be a negative into a positive.

### 4. Standing Out in a Competitive Market:

In today's global job market, competition is fierce. Many qualified individuals are vying for the same roles, which means that to stand out, you need to bring more than just a good CV. A great interview can set you apart from equally qualified candidates by showing that you are not just competent, but also a good communicator, a quick thinker, and someone who is genuinely excited about the opportunity.

*Example*: Two candidates might have similar technical skills, but the one who demonstrates enthusiasm for the company's vision and asks thoughtful, insightful questions will likely leave a more favourable impression than the one who simply answers questions without engaging deeply with the interviewer.

### 5. Building Relationships and Networks:

An interview is more than just a test of your qualifications. It's also an opportunity to build a relationship with your prospective employer. Even if you don't get the job, a strong interview performance can leave a lasting positive impression, which might lead to future opportunities. Good interview skills enable you to create rapport, show respect for the interviewer's time, and engage in a meaningful dialogue about the role and the organisation. Employers often remember candidates who were personable, thoughtful, and easy to talk to, even if they weren't the right fit at that moment.

*Example*: A candidate who asks smart, well researched questions about the company's future or the team's goals is likely to be remembered fondly by the interviewer, which could open doors later down the line, even if that specific role isn't offered.

### 6. Handling Rejection with Grace:

Not every interview will result in a job offer, but every interview is an opportunity to learn and grow. Strong interview skills help you to handle the process with grace, even if you don't get the desired outcome. You'll know how to reflect on your performance, gather feedback, and use that information to improve for future opportunities.

*Example*: Following a rejection, a candidate with solid interview skills may send a polite thank you note, leaving a positive impression and possibly keeping themselves in mind for future roles at the company.

### The Transformational Power of Interviews

Mastering interview skills is not just about securing a job; it's about developing the ability to sell your story, your achievements, and your potential. As the old adage goes, "You never get a second chance to make a first impression," and this is especially true in interviews. The more skilled you become at navigating these conversations, the more confident you'll be in pursuing career opportunities, negotiating job offers, and advancing professionally.

Great interview skills transform how you're perceived by employers, enabling you to showcase your strengths, connect on a personal level, and leave a lasting impression. This book will guide you through the strategies and techniques necessary to master the interview process, giving you the tools to thrive in any professional setting.

**Common Challenges and Misconceptions**

Interviews can be daunting, and many candidates face obstacles that prevent them from performing at their best. These challenges often stem from misconceptions about what an interview entails or from a lack of preparation. Understanding these common pitfalls is the first step toward overcoming them and mastering the art of interviews.

**1. Challenge: Thinking the Interview Is Only About Skills**

**Misconception:** "If I have the right qualifications, I'll get the job."

While qualifications are crucial, interviews are not just about ticking off skills on a checklist. Employers are also evaluating your personality, cultural fit, and soft skills, such as communication and teamwork. Many candidates assume that as long as their CV reflects the necessary qualifications, they can simply list them off in the interview. In reality, interviews are about much more than technical competence.

*Example*: A software developer might have excellent coding skills, but if they cannot communicate effectively, collaborate with team members, or present ideas clearly, they may be overlooked for a less technically skilled candidate who excels in those areas.

**Solution:** Understand that interviews are holistic. Prepare to demonstrate not only your skills but also how you work with others, handle challenges, and fit into the company culture. You need to show you are a well-rounded candidate.

## 2. Challenge: Over-preparation Leading to Over-rehearsal

**Misconception:** "I need to memorise perfect answers to every question."

While preparation is critical, some candidates fall into the trap of over-rehearsing their responses to the point where they sound robotic or insincere. Interviewers want to see genuine, thoughtful answers that show you've considered the question, rather than rehearsed scripts that lack authenticity. Over rehearsed answers can make you seem inflexible, and if an unexpected question comes up, you may be thrown off.

*Example*: A candidate who has memorised an answer to "Tell me about yourself" may sound stiff and unnatural if their response is too rigid or disconnected from the flow of conversation.

**Solution:** Instead of memorising exact answers, focus on understanding the key points you want to convey. Be flexible and adapt to the flow of the interview. Think of interviews as conversations, not exams. Practice, but aim to remain natural and responsive.

## 3. Challenge: Failing to Prepare for Behavioural Questions

**Misconception:** "The interviewer will only ask me about my previous roles and skills."

Many candidates assume the interview will focus solely on their technical qualifications and past job experiences. However, interviewers often use behavioural questions to assess how you've handled real-life work situations. These questions can catch unprepared candidates off guard, leading to vague or incomplete answers.

*Example*: A common behavioural question might be, "Tell me about a time you faced a difficult challenge at work." If you haven't prepared examples in advance, it's easy to stumble through your response.

**Solution:** Familiarise yourself with the STAR method (Situation, Task, Action, Result) and prepare specific examples from your past experiences. These should demonstrate your ability to solve problems, collaborate with others, or manage pressure effectively.

**4. Challenge: Believing Interviews Are One-Sided**

**Misconception:** "I just have to answer their questions and that's it."

Many candidates believe that an interview is a passive experience where the employer asks questions and the candidate responds. In reality, interviews are a two way conversation. Candidates who don't engage by asking insightful questions may come across as uninterested or uninformed about the role or company.

*Example*: At the end of an interview, when asked if they have any questions, a candidate who responds with, "No, you've answered everything" misses an opportunity to learn more about the company and showcase their curiosity.

**Solution:** Prepare a list of thoughtful questions that demonstrate your genuine interest in the role and the organisation. This shows that you're not just focused on getting the job but also considering how the company aligns with your goals and values. Questions like "How do you define success in this role?" or "Can you tell me more about the team I would be working with?" can set you apart.

## 5. Challenge: Letting Nerves Get the Best of You

**Misconception:** "Everyone else feels confident; I'm the only one nervous."

Interview anxiety is extremely common, yet many candidates believe they're the only ones struggling with nerves. This can make them feel inadequate or lead to self-sabotaging behaviours such as speaking too quickly, forgetting key points, or failing to engage fully with the interviewer.

*Example*: A candidate might be so nervous about answering questions that they fail to actively listen to the interviewer, missing critical cues or opportunities to build rapport.

**Solution:** Understand that nerves are normal. Practise relaxation techniques, such as deep breathing, before the interview. Also, remind yourself that the interview is a two way process you're assessing the company as much as they're assessing you. The more you practise interviews, the more comfortable you will become.

## 6. Challenge: Focusing Too Much on the Job Rather Than the Employer

**Misconception:** "If I'm the best fit for the job, I'll get it."

Many candidates focus exclusively on their ability to do the job itself, ignoring the broader context of the company's culture, values, and long term goals. Employers are looking for candidates who not only have the skills for the role but who also align with the company's ethos and mission. Focusing too much on the technical aspects of the job, without showing an interest in the company's vision or goals, can hurt your chances.

*Example*: A candidate might excel in explaining how they would perform specific tasks but fail to express why they're excited to join the company or how their values align with the company's mission.

**Solution:** Research the company thoroughly. Understand their values, recent achievements, and long term objectives. During the interview, show that you're not just interested in the job but also in being part of the company's future. Demonstrate enthusiasm for their mission, culture, and the role's potential contribution to that vision.

**7. Challenge: Assuming You're the Only One Under Scrutiny**

**Misconception:** "I'm the one being judged, so I have to prove myself."

It's easy to think that the interviewer holds all the power, but candidates often forget that they're also evaluating the company. This misconception can lead to a passive, deferential approach where the candidate feels they need to impress the interviewer at all costs. However, interviews should be mutually beneficial, where both sides assess if the relationship is a good fit.

*Example*: A candidate might accept any offer that comes their way, only to realise later that the company's culture or expectations don't align with their personal or professional goals.

**Solution:** Shift your mindset. Remember that an interview is as much about finding the right fit for you as it is for the employer. Be curious, ask thoughtful questions about the company's culture, management style, and expectations. This way, you'll make a more informed decision and find a role that truly suits your needs.

By addressing these common challenges and misconceptions, you can prepare for interviews more strategically and avoid many of the pitfalls that prevent candidates from succeeding. Knowing the reality behind these myths will not only boost your confidence but also enable you to approach interviews with clarity, poise, and authenticity.

**How Interviews Have Evolved in Today's Job Market**

The process of interviewing has undergone significant transformations in recent years, driven by technological advancements, shifts in workplace culture, and the growing complexity of the global job market. What was once a more straightforward exchange between a hiring manager and a candidate has evolved into a multi-faceted process designed to assess not only skills and qualifications but also values, cultural fit, and adaptability to modern work environments. Understanding how interviews have changed will help candidates better navigate the interview landscape and maximise their chances of success.

**1. The Rise of Remote and Virtual Interviews**

One of the most notable changes in the interview process is the widespread use of virtual interviews, particularly since the COVID-19 pandemic. Video platforms like Zoom, Microsoft Teams, and Google Meet have become the norm for first round interviews, and sometimes even the entire hiring process. This shift to virtual interviewing has allowed companies to broaden their talent pool, conducting interviews with candidates from different cities, countries, or continents.

**What This Means for Candidates:**

- You need to be proficient with video conferencing technology and ensure you have a reliable internet connection, as technical issues can derail a good interview.

- Body language and presentation are still key, even in a virtual setting. Eye contact (through the camera), good lighting, and a professional background can significantly affect how you're perceived.

- While virtual interviews can be more convenient, they also require a greater focus on communication skills, as subtle in person cues may be harder to convey or interpret online.

## 2. Competency-Based and Behavioural Interviews

Interviews have shifted from merely focusing on qualifications and experience to a deeper examination of *how* candidates handle real world situations. Competency based and behavioural interviews are now a common approach, where employers use questions designed to elicit examples of past behaviour to predict future performance.

These interviews often rely on the STAR method (Situation, Task, Action, Result) to assess how candidates have demonstrated specific competencies such as teamwork, leadership, problem-solving, or dealing with conflict. Employers are increasingly interested in how candidates behave in certain situations rather than just their technical abilities.

**What This Means for Candidates:**

- You should be prepared to answer behavioural questions by reflecting on your previous work experiences and crafting clear, concise stories that showcase your abilities.

- It's important to highlight the outcome of your actions and what you learned from each experience, demonstrating your growth and problem solving capabilities.
- Competency-based questions also test your soft skills employers want to know not just what you can do, but how you work with others, handle pressure, and adapt to challenges.

## 3. Increased Focus on Cultural Fit and Company Values

Modern companies are placing a greater emphasis on cultural fit, ensuring that candidates not only have the right skills but also align with the company's values and mission. This shift has been driven by a growing recognition that the best hires are not just those who can do the job, but those who will thrive in the company's specific environment.

Hiring managers now ask questions to assess a candidate's emotional intelligence, adaptability, and ability to collaborate with diverse teams. They also want to know how well a candidate's personal and professional values align with the company's culture and goals.

### What This Means for Candidates:

- Researching the company's culture, values, and mission is critical before an interview. This information will help you tailor your responses and demonstrate that you're not just interested in the role, but also excited to be part of the company's larger vision.
- Be prepared to discuss how your own values align with the company's. For example, if the company values innovation, share examples of times you've contributed to creative problem-solving or embraced new ideas.

- Companies are looking for employees who can be advocates for their culture, so showing genuine enthusiasm for their ethos can set you apart from other candidates.

## 4. The Emergence of Structured and Data-Driven Interviews

Many companies are now using structured interviews, where each candidate is asked the same set of predetermined questions to reduce bias and ensure fairness in the hiring process. This approach allows employers to standardise the evaluation process and use data-driven insights to compare candidates objectively.

In some industries, interviews may also include data driven assessments, such as psychometric testing, cognitive ability tests, or personality assessments. These tools provide additional insight into a candidate's potential fit and help companies predict job performance more accurately.

**What This Means for Candidates:**

- Be ready for a more formal interview process, where your responses will be directly compared to a set of predetermined criteria. Practising responses to common interview questions can help you prepare for this structured format.

- You might also encounter tests or assessments that measure your cognitive skills, personality traits, or even emotional intelligence. Familiarising yourself with the types of assessments used in your industry can give you an edge.

- These data driven methods are designed to uncover your problem solving abilities, creativity, and how you work under pressure, so be prepared to demonstrate these qualities both in interviews and any accompanying assessments.

## 5. The Blending of Traditional and Situational Interviews

Many employers now blend traditional interviews with situational or case based interviews. In a situational interview, you'll be asked to respond to hypothetical scenarios or problems you might face in the role. These questions are designed to assess your critical thinking, decision-making, and creativity in real time.

In certain industries like consulting, finance, or technology, you might be given a case study or practical task to work through during the interview. This form of assessment allows employers to see how you approach complex problems, think on your feet, and apply your expertise in a practical setting.

**What This Means for Candidates:**

- Practise answering situational questions by imagining how you'd respond to common challenges in the industry or role you're applying for. Be prepared to think on your feet and explain your reasoning step-by-step.

- In case based interviews, you'll need to demonstrate analytical thinking, but also your ability to communicate your thought process clearly. Even if you don't arrive at a perfect solution, showing a methodical approach can impress interviewers.

- Employers want to know not just what you think, but *how* you think. So, be transparent about your approach and demonstrate adaptability when faced with new information or unexpected challenges.

## 6. The Importance of Diversity, Equity, and Inclusion (DEI)

Today, more companies are focusing on creating diverse, equitable, and inclusive workplaces, and this is reflected in their interview processes.

Employers are now asking candidates how they've contributed to diversity and inclusion efforts in previous roles, or how they'd promote a positive, inclusive work environment.

Additionally, interview panels are often more diverse, and many companies now use DEI focused questions to ensure candidates will help foster a welcoming, respectful workplace for all employees.

**What This Means for Candidates:**

- Be prepared to answer questions about how you've supported diversity and inclusion in previous roles, even if indirectly. You might discuss how you've worked with diverse teams or promoted an inclusive work environment.

- Research the company's DEI policies and be ready to show how your own values align with their commitment to inclusion.

- Demonstrating awareness of and commitment to DEI issues can be a significant advantage, especially in industries where creating a diverse workplace is a key priority.

### 7. Follow-up and Feedback: A Growing Trend

Companies today are more transparent about their hiring processes, and many now provide candidates with structured feedback after interviews, even if they don't get the job. This trend is part of a larger shift towards improving the candidate experience, making interviews less opaque and more of a learning opportunity for those involved.

**What This Means for Candidates:**

- Expect follow up emails or feedback if you're not selected. If feedback is provided, use it to improve your performance in future interviews.

- Asking for feedback can also demonstrate professionalism and a willingness to improve, making you stand out even if you're not selected for the current role.

The modern interview process is dynamic, sophisticated, and increasingly focused on finding candidates who are not only technically capable but also adaptable, culturally aligned, and forward thinking. As you navigate these evolving trends, remember that mastering interview skills requires not only preparation but also flexibility in adjusting to the changing landscape of today's job market.

## Chapter 1: Preparing Like a Pro

### Researching the Company and Role

Preparation is the cornerstone of interview success, and one of the most important aspects of preparation is researching the company and the role you're applying for. While this might sound obvious, too many candidates underestimate the depth of research needed to truly stand out in an interview. It's not enough to skim through the company's website or read a job description; thorough research allows you to demonstrate genuine interest, ask intelligent questions, and present yourself as a well-informed candidate who understands both the company and the role. Let's explore how to approach this crucial step effectively.

### 1. Understanding the Company's Core Mission and Values

Every company has a unique mission and set of values that guide its operations, decisions, and culture. These core principles often form the backbone of what the company stands for and what it expects from its employees. Companies seek candidates who resonate with their mission and align with their values, so having a clear understanding of these elements will set you apart from other applicants.

**How to Research:**

- **Company Website:** Start by visiting the "About Us" section of the company's website. This will often provide key insights into the company's history, mission statement, and values. Pay attention to how they describe their purpose and the language they use this can give you clues about their organisational culture.

- **Annual Reports or Press Releases:** Many companies publish annual reports or press releases that give deeper insight into their goals, successes, and challenges. These can often be found on the company's website or through public financial reporting channels. Understanding the company's recent achievements and long-term strategy allows you to connect your skills and experiences to their current objectives.

- **Social Media and Blog Posts:** Company blogs and social media channels can provide a more informal, but equally valuable, perspective. These platforms often highlight current initiatives, workplace culture, and the company's interaction with the broader community.

**Example:** If you're interviewing for a company that places a strong emphasis on sustainability and ethical business practices, you should be prepared to explain how your personal values and past work experiences align with those goals. You could mention any environmentally friendly practices you've incorporated into your work or talk about volunteer efforts that reflect your commitment to similar causes.

## 2. Studying the Industry and Competitors

Employers want candidates who are knowledgeable not only about the company but also about the wider industry in which it operates. Understanding industry trends, challenges, and competitors shows that you have a broader awareness of the market and that you're serious about contributing to the company's success.

**How to Research:**

- **Industry News:** Subscribe to industry-specific newsletters or visit reputable websites that provide news and updates about the sector. This will keep you informed about current trends, regulatory changes, or technological advancements that might affect the company.

- **Competitor Analysis:** Research key competitors in the market. What are they doing differently? How does your prospective employer stand out against them? This will not only help you demonstrate your industry knowledge but will also allow you to highlight ways in which the company you're applying to can leverage its strengths in the market.

**Example:** Imagine you're interviewing for a role in a fast-moving consumer goods (FMCG) company. By researching industry trends, you might learn that sustainability and eco-friendly packaging are growing concerns. You could use this information to discuss how the company's competitors are responding to these trends and suggest ideas for how the company you're interviewing with could innovate in this area.

## 3. Diving Deep into the Job Description

The job description is your blueprint for the role, but it's important to go beyond simply reading it.

A deep analysis of the job posting can help you better understand the company's expectations and allow you to tailor your responses in the interview to meet those expectations. The goal is to read between the lines and anticipate what the employer is truly looking for in a candidate.

**How to Research:**

- **Break Down the Job Requirements:** Look at the skills and qualifications listed in the job description. Make a list of these requirements and reflect on how your experience aligns with each one. Think of specific examples from your past roles that demonstrate your ability to fulfil these duties.

- **Identify the Employer's Pain Points:** Job descriptions often provide clues about the challenges the company is facing. For example, if a job posting emphasises a need for "strong problem-solving skills" or "experience with rapid scaling," it could indicate that the company is experiencing growing pains or struggling with internal inefficiencies. Understanding these underlying challenges allows you to address them directly in the interview.

**Example:** If a job description lists "experience with managing cross-functional teams" as a requirement, consider not only the instances in which you've led teams but also what specific challenges you faced and overcame. Did you streamline communication across departments? Did you resolve conflicts effectively? Preparing concrete examples will demonstrate that you have the experience to back up your claims.

## 4. Researching the Company's Leadership and Key Employees

Employers want to know that you're engaged with the company's vision and culture, and one way to demonstrate this is by learning about the leadership team and key employees. Understanding who the company's leaders are, their background, and their vision for the company shows that you're invested in the future of the organisation. This also helps you tailor your interview responses to the specific needs and goals of those you'll be working with.

**How to Research:**

- **LinkedIn:** Explore the LinkedIn profiles of the company's leadership team and key figures within the department you're applying to. Take note of their career paths, key achievements, and any shared connections or affiliations.

- **Interviews and Public Talks:** Look for interviews, podcasts, or public talks given by the company's executives. This can give you insight into their management style, long-term goals, and the qualities they value in employees.

**Example:** If the CEO has recently spoken about expanding into new markets, you can mention this in the interview and discuss how your international experience could support this objective. This not only demonstrates that you've done your homework but also shows that you're thinking proactively about how you can contribute to the company's goals.

## 5. Understanding the Company Culture

Company culture plays a significant role in employee satisfaction and retention, and hiring managers want to ensure that new hires will thrive within the company's environment.

Whether the company has a casual, start-up-like culture or a more traditional corporate atmosphere, understanding their working environment will help you assess if it's a good fit for you and give you the opportunity to tailor your answers to align with their culture.

**How to Research:**

- **Glassdoor and Employee Reviews:** Sites like Glassdoor offer insights into what current and former employees think about the company. You can learn about the work-life balance, management style, and overall employee satisfaction. However, take these reviews with a grain of caution, as they may represent extreme experiences.

- **Company Blog or Newsroom:** The tone and content of a company's blog can give you a sense of their internal culture. For instance, if the company frequently writes about employee wellness, work-life balance, or diversity initiatives, this can tell you that they prioritise those values.

**Example:** Suppose the company has a culture of collaboration and innovation. During the interview, you could highlight examples of times you worked in cross functional teams or contributed to innovative projects, framing your experience in a way that resonates with the company's values.

### 6. Preparing Thoughtful Questions

Part of researching the company and the role involves preparing thoughtful questions that reflect your interest and engagement. Interviews are two way conversations, and asking insightful questions shows that you're thinking critically about how you can contribute to the company.

**How to Prepare:**

- **Role-Specific Questions:** Ask about the challenges the department is facing or what success looks like in the role. This shows that you're already thinking about how you'll perform and contribute.

- **Company-Specific Questions:** Inquire about the company's long-term goals or how they are addressing industry trends. This demonstrates that you're not just interested in the role but also in the company's future.

**Example:** You could ask, "I read that your company recently expanded into new markets. How do you see this impacting the team's objectives over the next year?" This question shows that you're paying attention to the company's growth and are already thinking about how you can help meet their objectives.

By thoroughly researching the company and the role, you're not just preparing to answer questions you're positioning yourself as a candidate who understands the business, its challenges, and its future. This level of preparation reflects a level of commitment and insight that will make you stand out from the competition and demonstrate that you're ready to contribute from day one.

**Understanding Job Descriptions and Tailoring Responses**

A job description is far more than a list of tasks; it's the key to understanding what an employer is really looking for in a candidate. Successful interview preparation involves thoroughly analysing the job description, identifying the underlying skills and qualities sought by the employer, and crafting responses that highlight how you meet (and exceed) those requirements. Tailoring your answers to align with the job description shows the employer that you've done your homework and that you're an ideal fit for the role.

## 1. Breaking Down the Job Description

A typical job description includes several sections such as responsibilities, required qualifications, skills, and sometimes a company overview. Each of these sections provides valuable information that helps you tailor your responses effectively.

**Key Sections to Focus On:**

- **Responsibilities and Duties:** This section outlines the day-to-day tasks the role entails. Look for keywords like "manage," "coordinate," "develop," or "lead" to understand what is expected of you.

- **Required Skills and Qualifications:** Employers will list the essential skills, education, and experience they want. While you don't have to tick every single box, identifying which qualifications are non-negotiable and which are flexible is crucial for tailoring your answers.

- **Preferred Qualifications:** These are nice to have qualities that set candidates apart. If you possess any of these skills, make sure to highlight them, as they can give you an edge.

- **Soft Skills:** Soft skills are often mentioned implicitly or explicitly in job descriptions, such as teamwork, communication, problem solving, and leadership. Identify the specific interpersonal qualities the company is seeking.

**Example:** If a job description says, "Collaborate with cross-functional teams to deliver product innovations," you'll want to prepare examples of times when you've worked with multiple departments or teams. You'll need to show not just that you can handle the technical aspects, but also that you can effectively communicate and collaborate.

## 2. Identifying Key Skills and Competencies

One of the most important steps in preparing for an interview is recognising the core competencies the employer is looking for. Many job descriptions include a mix of hard and soft skills, and understanding the balance between the two can help you tailor your responses to highlight the right attributes.

**Hard Skills:** These are the technical abilities and knowledge required for the role, such as proficiency in software, coding languages, or financial modelling. These are often explicitly stated in the job description.

**Soft Skills:** These refer to more general, interpersonal abilities, like communication, teamwork, or adaptability. They are sometimes stated explicitly or implied within phrases like "must be a strong team player" or "able to work in a fast-paced environment."

**Example:** If a job posting for a project manager mentions "strong leadership" and "budget management," you'll want to prepare examples where you demonstrated leadership in managing a project successfully while keeping costs within budget. The goal is to showcase both your ability to lead a team and your financial acumen.

## 3. Reading Between the Lines

Job descriptions are often written in general terms, but they contain subtle clues about the company's pain points and priorities. The language used can help you discern what the employer is truly seeking and how to position yourself as the solution to their challenges.

**Common Clues to Look For:**

- **Emphasis on Time Management:** Words like "fast-paced" or "must handle multiple projects" indicate that the company values efficiency and expects you to juggle multiple tasks. Tailor your responses to demonstrate your ability to meet tight deadlines or manage competing priorities.

- **Focus on Growth and Innovation:** If the company talks about "innovation" or "scaling rapidly," it signals that they're looking for someone comfortable with change and capable of driving growth. Share examples where you've contributed to innovation or helped a company scale.

- **Team Oriented Language:** If the job description emphasises collaboration or teamwork, such as "work with diverse teams," you'll need to demonstrate your ability to work well with others and your experience in cross-functional roles.

**Example:** Imagine a job description states, "The ideal candidate will thrive in a high pressure, dynamic environment." This suggests the company wants someone resilient, adaptable, and quick to solve problems. When answering interview questions, focus on examples where you succeeded despite pressure, or explain how you remain calm and efficient in fast-moving situations.

### 4. Aligning Your Experience with the Job Description

Once you've broken down the job description, it's time to align your experience with what the employer is looking for. The key is to translate your previous roles and experiences into language that fits the needs and expectations of the current position. This involves matching your skills and experiences with the job description's requirements.

**Steps to Align Your Experience:**

- **Map Your Experiences to the Role:** For each major requirement in the job description, find a corresponding experience from your past roles. Be ready to provide specific examples using the STAR method (Situation, Task, Action, Result).

- **Use Keywords from the Job Description:** Rephrase your answers using keywords from the job description itself. This reinforces the connection between your qualifications and the role.

- **Tailor Your Achievements:** Focus on accomplishments that are directly relevant to the job. Even if you have impressive achievements, if they don't align with the role, they won't resonate as strongly.

**Example:** If you're applying for a sales manager position and the job description highlights the need for "increased revenue generation," your response could be, "In my previous role, I increased regional sales by 25% through implementing new lead generation strategies and improving client relationships." This directly addresses the employer's priorities and shows measurable success.

## 5. Crafting Tailored Responses for Common Interview Questions

Once you've identified the key elements in the job description, you can tailor your responses to common interview questions to reflect these priorities. Every response should reinforce your suitability for the specific role, drawing on both the job description and your past experience.

**Common Interview Questions to Tailor:**

- **"Tell me about yourself."** Tailor this answer by highlighting the experiences and skills most relevant to the job description. Briefly mention why you're interested in this particular role and how your background aligns with the company's goals.

- **"Why are you interested in this position?"** Show that you've done your homework by referencing specific aspects of the job description. Explain how your skills match the requirements and how you can contribute to the company's objectives.

- **"Can you give an example of a time you demonstrated [specific skill]?"** Use the job description to guide which examples you choose. If teamwork is heavily emphasised, provide an example that showcases your collaboration skills. If problem solving is key, share an example where you effectively resolved a difficult issue.

**Example:** If the job description states that they're looking for someone who "can lead large teams," and you're asked about your leadership experience, tailor your response to that expectation. You might say, "In my previous role as team lead, I managed a department of 15 employees, overseeing projects from initial planning through completion. By fostering open communication and delegating tasks based on individual strengths, I improved team productivity by 20% over a year."

### 6. Customising Your Questions for the Employer

Tailoring your responses also means customising the questions you ask the interviewer. Use the job description as a springboard to ask thoughtful questions that demonstrate your genuine interest in the role and the company's challenges.

**Examples of Customised Questions:**

- "The job description mentioned that this role involves cross-departmental collaboration. Can you tell me more about how teams typically work together here?"

- "I noticed that the role emphasises scaling the business. What are the company's current priorities in terms of growth, and how would this role contribute to that?"

- "The job posting highlights innovation. Could you provide some examples of how your team has recently driven innovation within the company?"

These types of questions not only show that you've thoroughly read and understood the job description but also give you a deeper insight into how the company operates.

### 7. Bringing It All Together

Understanding the job description and tailoring your responses is a multi-step process that involves deep analysis, critical thinking, and alignment between your experience and the employer's needs. By demonstrating that you've thoroughly researched the position and tailored your answers to match the role, you'll stand out as a thoughtful and well-prepared candidate.

**Final Tips:**

- **Revisit the Job Description Frequently:** As you prepare for your interview, keep revisiting the job description. With each re-read, you'll identify new details that can enhance your preparation.

- **Practice Tailored Responses:** Prepare and rehearse responses that incorporate the job description's key elements. Practising in advance will ensure you deliver your answers confidently.

- **Stay Flexible:** While you should tailor your answers, avoid rigidly sticking to one set of responses. Be flexible and responsive to the flow of the interview, ensuring you adjust based on the specific direction it takes.

By carefully aligning your responses with the job description, you position yourself as the candidate who not only meets the basic requirements but also brings added value and insight to the role.

**Practising Common Interview Questions**

Preparation is key to a successful interview, and one of the most effective ways to prepare is by practising answers to common interview questions. Employers tend to ask a blend of standard questions, and having well-crafted responses allows you to highlight your skills, experience, and personality in a concise and compelling manner. The goal isn't to memorise scripted answers, but rather to practice articulating thoughtful, tailored responses that show you are well-prepared and confident.

**1. The Importance of Practising Interview Questions**

Practising your responses to common interview questions helps you in several ways. First, it helps you avoid being caught off guard by unexpected questions and allows you to deliver more structured, clear answers. It also reduces anxiety, as familiarity with the types of questions asked boosts your confidence and ability to think on your feet. Moreover, practising helps you refine your answers, ensuring you showcase the most relevant aspects of your experience and skills.

## 2. The STAR Method for Structuring Responses

One of the most effective ways to structure answers to competency-based or behavioural interview questions is by using the STAR method: **Situation, Task, Action,** and **Result**. This technique ensures your responses are organised and focused on showcasing both your problem-solving abilities and the positive outcomes of your actions.

- **Situation:** Set the context for your example. Explain a specific challenge or circumstance you faced.
- **Task:** Describe your responsibility or goal in the situation.
- **Action:** Explain what steps you took to address the challenge or complete the task.
- **Result:** Share the outcome of your actions, ideally with measurable results or improvements.

**Example:** *Question:* "Can you give an example of how you handled a difficult situation at work?" *Response (using STAR):*

- **Situation:** "In my previous role as a customer service manager, we had a period where customer complaints about delayed orders spiked due to a system error."
- **Task:** "I was responsible for calming frustrated customers and resolving their issues as quickly as possible."
- **Action:** "I introduced a temporary manual tracking system, set up a dedicated team to monitor delayed orders, and ensured that customers were informed of the status of their orders regularly."
- **Result:** "Within two weeks, we reduced complaint calls by 40%, and customer satisfaction scores improved by 15%."

## 3. Common Interview Questions and How to Practise Them

Here are some of the most frequently asked interview questions, along with guidance on how to structure your answers.

### a) "Tell me about yourself."

This is often the opening question in an interview, and it's your opportunity to make a strong first impression. Employers want a concise overview of your professional background and how it relates to the position you're applying for. You should tailor this answer to focus on your most relevant experiences and skills, rather than offering a detailed life story.

**How to Practise:**

- Keep your answer focused on your career path, key achievements, and how your experience aligns with the role.
- Highlight skills or experiences that directly relate to the job description.

**Example:** "I have over five years of experience in project management, with a focus on streamlining operations and improving team collaboration. In my last role, I successfully led a team of 10 to complete a product launch that increased our market share by 12%. I'm excited about this role because it aligns with my passion for driving efficiency and leading high-performing teams."

### b) "Why are you interested in this role?"

This question assesses how well you've researched the company and the position. Your answer should demonstrate not only your knowledge of the role but also how your goals align with the company's mission, culture, and future plans.

**How to Practise:**

- Mention specific elements of the job description that excite you.
- Explain how your skills can contribute to the company's success.

**Example:** "I'm particularly excited about this role because of the opportunity to work with innovative technologies in the healthcare sector. I've followed your company's recent advancements in medical software, and my experience in software development, coupled with my passion for improving patient outcomes, makes this a perfect fit."

### c) "What are your strengths?"

This is your chance to highlight your key strengths, particularly those that match the job description. Avoid vague answers like "I'm a hard worker." Instead, focus on specific strengths and provide examples of how they've contributed to your success in previous roles.

**How to Practise:**

- Choose 2–3 strengths that align with the job requirements.
- Provide examples of how these strengths have helped you achieve positive outcomes.

**Example:** "One of my key strengths is my attention to detail. In my previous role as a financial analyst, I identified discrepancies in budgeting reports that saved the company over £50,000 in potential losses. I'm also highly organised, which helps me manage multiple projects simultaneously without compromising on quality."

### d) "What are your weaknesses?"

Employers ask this question to assess self-awareness and your ability to work on areas of improvement. Avoid clichés like "I'm a perfectionist." Instead, be honest about a weakness, and importantly, focus on the steps you're taking to address it.

**How to Practise:**

- Choose a real, but not critical, weakness.
- Explain how you are actively working to improve it.

**Example:** "I used to struggle with delegation, as I preferred to handle tasks myself to ensure they were done correctly. However, I've been actively working on improving this by trusting my team and providing clear guidance. In fact, I've noticed that delegating effectively has increased team productivity and morale."

### e) "Can you tell me about a time you faced a challenge at work and how you handled it?"

This behavioural question requires a specific example from your past experience. Employers are looking to see how you approach problems, work under pressure, and find solutions.

**How to Practise:**

- Use the STAR method to structure your answer.
- Choose a relevant example that showcases your problem-solving abilities.

**Example:** "In my previous role, we experienced a major software glitch during a product launch that could have delayed the project.

I quickly gathered the team, identified the root cause, and worked with our IT department to implement a workaround within 48 hours. As a result, we launched the product on time and without any impact on our customers."

### f) "Where do you see yourself in five years?"

This question assesses your long-term goals and whether they align with the company's vision. Your answer should reflect both ambition and a commitment to growing within the company.

**How to Practise:**

- Mention professional goals that align with the role and the company's trajectory.
- Show enthusiasm for growing with the company.

**Example:** "In five years, I see myself taking on greater leadership responsibilities within this organisation, potentially managing larger teams or spearheading major projects. I'm eager to develop my skills further and contribute to the long-term growth of the company."

### g) "Why should we hire you?"

This question is your opportunity to close the deal. Your answer should summarise why you're the best candidate for the role by aligning your strengths, experience, and enthusiasm with the company's needs.

**How to Practise:**

- Highlight how your skills match the key requirements of the role.
- Focus on the unique value you bring to the team.

**Example:** "You should hire me because I bring a proven track record of delivering results under pressure. My experience in [specific skill relevant to the job] aligns perfectly with your needs, and I'm confident that my skills in [another key area] will help drive the success of your team. Additionally, I'm passionate about your company's mission and excited to contribute to its growth."

### 4. Mock Interviews and Feedback

One of the best ways to practise is by participating in mock interviews. Whether you practise with a friend, mentor, or even record yourself, mock interviews allow you to rehearse your answers in a realistic setting. After the mock interview, seek feedback on your answers, tone, body language, and clarity.

**Tips for Effective Mock Interviews:**

- Simulate a real interview environment by dressing professionally and timing your responses.

- Ask your mock interviewer to throw in some unexpected questions to test your ability to think on your feet.

- After the interview, review what went well and what areas need improvement.

### 5. The Role of Confidence and Adaptability

Practising common interview questions isn't just about memorising answers it's about building confidence and adaptability. By rehearsing your responses, you'll be able to answer questions more naturally and adjust to any variations that come your way. Interviews often deviate from the script, so having a flexible approach will allow you to respond calmly and clearly, even when faced with unexpected questions.

In conclusion, practising common interview questions is an essential step in your interview preparation. It helps you refine your answers, boosts your confidence, and ensures that you can clearly communicate your strengths and suitability for the role. Through thoughtful practice, you'll be able to present yourself as a prepared, knowledgeable, and enthusiastic candidate.

## Importance of Personal Branding and Your Value Proposition

In today's competitive job market, your personal brand and value proposition play a crucial role in distinguishing you from other candidates. While your qualifications, skills, and experience are essential, how you present yourself and your personal brand can significantly influence how potential employers perceive you. Your value proposition, on the other hand, encapsulates the unique value you bring to an organisation and why they should hire you over someone else. Together, personal branding and a strong value proposition help create a memorable impression and effectively communicate your worth to employers.

### 1. What is Personal Branding?

Personal branding is the process of creating a cohesive and consistent image of who you are professionally. It encompasses your skills, experience, personality, and values and how these are communicated through your actions, reputation, and public persona. In essence, it's how you market yourself to employers, clients, and colleagues.

A strong personal brand goes beyond your CV and interview performance. It involves cultivating a professional image across all touchpoints, including your online presence (LinkedIn, personal websites, etc.), communication style, and even your appearance during interviews. Your brand should reflect your strengths, core values, and the qualities that set you apart.

**Example:** If you're a marketing professional with a reputation for creativity and innovative campaigns, your personal brand could focus on being a forward thinking marketer who pushes the boundaries of traditional marketing approaches to deliver impactful results.

### 2. Why Personal Branding Matters in Interviews

In an interview, your personal brand helps convey a consistent message about who you are and what you stand for. While many candidates may have similar qualifications, your brand differentiates you and makes you memorable. Employers are not just looking for someone who can do the job they're looking for someone who fits with the company culture and can add value beyond just the technical skills.

A well-defined personal brand can:

- **Establish Credibility:** It showcases your expertise and demonstrates that you are confident and knowledgeable in your field.

- **Communicate Consistency:** It helps you present a clear and consistent narrative about your professional journey, making it easier for employers to understand your career progression and future potential.

- **Build Trust:** Employers are more likely to trust someone who has a well established reputation, both online and offline.

- **Enhance Professional Presence:** Your brand shapes how you present yourself in interviews how you speak, how you answer questions, and how you interact with others in a professional setting.

**Example:** If your personal brand focuses on being a problem-solver with a customer centric approach, your answers in the interview should reinforce this by highlighting your ability to resolve client issues or improve customer satisfaction in previous roles.

### 3. What is a Value Proposition?

Your **value proposition** is a concise statement that communicates the unique value you bring to the table. It answers the critical question employers are asking: **Why should we hire you?** Your value proposition focuses on what makes you stand out and how your skills, experience, and strengths align with the needs of the company.

An effective value proposition:

- **Addresses Employer Needs:** It should directly reflect how you can solve the company's problems or meet its goals.

- **Highlights Unique Qualities:** It focuses on what sets you apart from other candidates, such as specialised skills, specific accomplishments, or unique experiences.

- **Is Clear and Concise:** A value proposition should be short and to the point, summarising your key strengths in a way that is easy to remember.

**Example of a Strong Value Proposition:** "As a data-driven marketing professional with a proven track record of increasing ROI by 20% through targeted digital campaigns, I can help your company optimise its marketing strategies and achieve greater profitability."

## 4. Developing Your Personal Brand and Value Proposition

Crafting a strong personal brand and value proposition requires self-awareness and reflection on your strengths, achievements, and career goals. The process involves understanding how others perceive you and intentionally shaping that perception to reflect the image you want to project.

### a) Defining Your Personal Brand

Start by asking yourself the following questions:

- **What are my core strengths?** These could be technical skills, soft skills, or industry expertise.

- **What am I passionate about?** Highlighting your passion adds depth to your brand and shows that you're driven by more than just financial gain.

- **What makes me unique?** This could be your specific experience, achievements, or your approach to problem-solving.

- **How do others perceive me?** Gather feedback from colleagues, supervisors, or clients to understand your existing brand and how it aligns with your desired image.

**Example:** If you've consistently been described as a natural leader with the ability to inspire teams, you can build your brand around leadership, team collaboration, and empowerment.

### b) Creating a Compelling Value Proposition

To develop your value proposition, focus on the following key areas:

- **Identify Employer Needs:** Study the job description and research the company to understand what challenges they face or what qualities they value in an employee.
- **Match Your Skills to Their Needs:** Highlight the skills and experiences you possess that align with the employer's priorities.
- **Quantify Your Achievements:** Whenever possible, use numbers or tangible outcomes to demonstrate the value you've delivered in previous roles.

**Example:** If a company is looking for someone to improve process efficiency, and you've previously implemented a system that reduced project timelines by 30%, this is the type of value you should feature in your value proposition.

## 5. Communicating Your Brand and Value Proposition in Interviews

Once you've developed your personal brand and value proposition, it's crucial to consistently communicate them throughout the interview process. Here are some strategies to ensure you're presenting yourself effectively:

### a) Integrate Your Value Proposition into Responses

When answering common interview questions, find ways to weave in your value proposition. This is especially important for questions like:

- "Tell me about yourself."
- "Why should we hire you?"
- "What are your strengths?"

Tailor your responses to focus on your unique value and how it aligns with the employer's needs. Every answer should reinforce the message of your personal brand.

**Example (Tell me about yourself):** "As a project manager with 7 years of experience in the IT sector, I have a proven track record of leading cross functional teams to deliver projects on time and within budget. My focus on clear communication and process optimisation has helped reduce project delivery times by 15% in my last two roles, and I'm excited about the opportunity to bring that expertise to your team."

### b) Present a Consistent Image Across All Touchpoints

Your personal brand should be consistent across every aspect of your professional life. This means ensuring that your:

- **LinkedIn Profile** reflects your key skills, achievements, and personal brand.

- **CV** is aligned with your brand and value proposition, highlighting accomplishments that support your narrative.

- **Professional Appearance and Demeanour** during interviews match the image you want to project.

**Example:** If your personal brand focuses on innovation and forward thinking, your CV, LinkedIn, and interview responses should highlight how you've driven innovation in past roles, and you should present yourself as a dynamic, adaptable professional.

### c) Use the STAR Method to Highlight Your Value

When answering behavioural questions, structure your responses using the STAR method to clearly demonstrate the value you bring.

Focus on how your unique approach, skills, and strengths resulted in positive outcomes, further reinforcing your personal brand and value proposition.

**Example (STAR Method - "Tell me about a time you solved a problem at work"):**

- **Situation:** "At my previous company, we faced a major bottleneck in our supply chain that delayed product deliveries by up to a week."
- **Task:** "As the logistics manager, it was my responsibility to streamline the process and reduce delays."
- **Action:** "I implemented a new inventory management system that tracked stock levels in real-time, allowing us to adjust orders and predict shortages more accurately."
- **Result:** "Within three months, we reduced delivery times by 30%, and customer satisfaction improved significantly."

## 6. Building a Long-Term Personal Brand

Your personal brand isn't static it evolves with your career and experiences. Continuously refine and develop your brand by:

- **Seeking Feedback:** Regularly ask for input from peers, supervisors, and mentors to ensure that your brand aligns with how others perceive you.
- **Staying Visible:** Maintain a strong professional presence by networking, attending industry events, and contributing to discussions in your field.
- **Showcasing Expertise:** Publish articles, give talks, or share insights on platforms like LinkedIn to demonstrate your thought leadership and expertise.

A well-crafted personal brand and value proposition not only increase your chances of success in interviews but also help you build a lasting professional reputation that will benefit your career in the long run.

**Conclusion**

In today's highly competitive job market, developing a strong personal brand and a compelling value proposition is essential for standing out from other candidates. By clearly articulating your strengths, experience, and unique value, you position yourself as the ideal candidate who not only meets the requirements but also brings something extra to the table. Whether you're answering common interview questions or engaging with employers online, consistency in your messaging will help you create a lasting, positive impression that sets you apart and increases your chances of landing the role you want.

**Chapter 2: Building Confidence**

**Mindset Techniques to Reduce Anxiety**

Job interviews can be nerve wracking, and it's common for even the most experienced professionals to feel a sense of anxiety. The good news is that your mindset plays a significant role in how you handle interview nerves. By mastering specific techniques to control anxiety, you can walk into an interview with confidence and clarity, ensuring that you're able to present the best version of yourself.

Let's explore several mindset techniques designed to help reduce interview anxiety and instil a calm, focused mindset.

## 1. Reframe Anxiety as Excitement

A simple yet effective way to manage interview anxiety is by reframing it. Research has shown that anxiety and excitement are physiologically similar emotions; both involve an elevated heart rate, heightened alertness, and a rush of adrenaline. Instead of interpreting those feelings as negative stress or fear, try to see them as signals of excitement. You are excited about the opportunity, excited to share your skills, and excited to engage with the interviewer.

**Technique in Action:** Before the interview, when you feel nervousness creeping in, tell yourself: "I'm excited about this opportunity" rather than "I'm anxious about the outcome." This small mental shift can trick your brain into seeing the situation in a more positive light, allowing you to channel that energy into a confident performance.

**Example:** Imagine you're about to give a presentation to a large audience. Rather than telling yourself you're anxious and fearful, remind yourself that you're excited to share your expertise and engage with others. This positive mindset can turn the nervous energy into enthusiasm.

## 2. Use Visualisation Techniques

Visualisation is a powerful tool used by top athletes, performers, and professionals to prepare for high pressure situations. The brain doesn't always differentiate between real experiences and imagined ones, which means vividly imagining a successful interview can help reduce anxiety and improve performance.

**How to Practise Visualisation:**

- **Find a Quiet Space:** Close your eyes and imagine yourself walking into the interview room, feeling calm and composed.

- **Visualise Success:** Picture yourself confidently answering questions, connecting with the interviewer, and presenting yourself as a strong candidate.

- **Focus on Positive Outcomes:** Imagine the interview ending on a positive note, with the interviewer impressed by your responses.

This exercise primes your brain for success by making the interview feel more familiar, thus reducing anxiety when the real moment arrives.

**Example:** If you're preparing for a job in sales, visualise yourself speaking confidently about your previous achievements, answering questions with ease, and having the interviewer nod in agreement. Picture the handshake at the end, knowing you made a lasting impression.

### 3. Breathing Exercises to Calm the Nervous System

One of the most effective ways to reduce immediate feelings of anxiety is through controlled breathing. When you're nervous, your breathing tends to become shallow and quick, which exacerbates feelings of anxiety. Deep breathing techniques activate the body's parasympathetic nervous system, which helps calm you down and reduce the physical symptoms of stress.

**Technique: 4-7-8 Breathing**

- **Inhale** deeply through your nose for 4 seconds.
- **Hold** your breath for 7 seconds.
- **Exhale** slowly through your mouth for 8 seconds.

Repeat this process several times before the interview to calm your mind and body. The focus on counting and breathing helps distract your mind from anxious thoughts while slowing your heart rate and calming your nervous system.

**Example:** Before entering the interview room, take a few minutes in a quiet space to practise 4-7-8 breathing. This will help you feel grounded and reduce the nervous tension that may have built up beforehand.

**4. Adopt a Growth Mindset**

A growth mindset is the belief that abilities and intelligence can be developed through effort and learning. Approaching an interview with a growth mindset allows you to see the experience as an opportunity for learning, rather than a test you must pass. This can reduce pressure and help alleviate anxiety because your self-worth is no longer tied to the outcome of a single interview.

**How to Shift to a Growth Mindset:**

- **Focus on the Process, Not the Outcome:** Instead of worrying about whether you'll get the job, focus on how well you can communicate your strengths and enjoy the conversation with the interviewer.
- **Embrace Challenges as Learning Opportunities:** Even if the interview doesn't go as planned, view it as a chance to learn and improve for next time. Every interview is valuable experience.

Adopting a growth mindset allows you to approach the interview with curiosity and a willingness to grow, reducing the overwhelming pressure to be perfect.

**Example:** If you're asked a difficult question during the interview that you struggle to answer, instead of panicking, remind yourself that this is an opportunity to learn. After the interview, reflect on what you could improve next time, rather than viewing the stumble as a failure.

### 5. Positive Affirmations and Self-Talk

The way you talk to yourself has a profound impact on your confidence and anxiety levels. Negative self-talk such as "I'm not qualified for this job" or "I always mess up interviews" can significantly increase feelings of anxiety. On the other hand, positive affirmations and self-talk can boost your confidence and calm your nerves.

**How to Practise Positive Affirmations:**

- **Create a List of Affirmations:** Write down positive statements about yourself and your abilities, such as:
    - "I am well prepared for this interview."
    - "I have the skills and experience to excel in this role."
    - "I handle challenges with confidence and ease."

- **Repeat These Affirmations:** Say these affirmations to yourself before the interview, either out loud or silently. This helps to build confidence and drown out any negative or self-doubting thoughts.

**Example:** If you begin to feel anxious during the interview, remind yourself internally, "I am qualified for this role, and I have the experience to succeed." This positive reinforcement can help you remain focused and composed.

## 6. Prepare for the Worst-Case Scenario

Sometimes, the fear of the unknown can fuel anxiety. To counter this, take a few minutes to think about the worst case scenario what's the worst that could happen in the interview? Often, when we face our fears head-on, we realise they're not as scary as they seem.

Once you've considered the worst-case scenario, ask yourself:

- **Is this outcome likely?** Often, the worst case scenario is highly unlikely or manageable.

- **How would I handle it?** Imagine yourself gracefully handling the worst case situation. For example, if you stumble on a question, picture yourself calmly saying, "I'd need to reflect more on that," and then smoothly moving on to the next topic.

By visualising how you'd respond to challenging situations, you gain a sense of control, which reduces feelings of anxiety.

**Example:** If you're nervous about forgetting important details during the interview, imagine yourself acknowledging the situation calmly. You might say, "Let me gather my thoughts for a moment," and then provide a clear response after a brief pause. This level of preparation helps to alleviate the fear of embarrassment or failure.

**7. Ground Yourself with Present Moment Awareness**

Anxiety often stems from worrying about future outcomes or ruminating on past mistakes. Grounding techniques help bring your focus back to the present moment, where you can take control of your thoughts and actions.

**Simple Grounding Techniques:**

- **Use Your Senses:** Before or during the interview, engage your senses by focusing on what you can see, hear, touch, taste, and smell. This brings your mind out of anxious "what if" scenarios and back to the present.

- **Focus on Your Feet:** If you start feeling overwhelmed during the interview, take a deep breath and focus on your feet touching the floor. Feel the ground supporting you. This helps anchor you in the moment and calms your racing thoughts.

**Example:** As you wait to be called into the interview room, instead of letting your mind spiral into anxiety, focus on the feeling of the chair you're sitting on, the temperature of the room, and the sound of people talking around you. This keeps you present and reduces nervousness.

**8. Create a Pre Interview Routine**

Having a consistent routine before an interview can help calm your mind and create a sense of familiarity and control. When you establish a pre-interview ritual, you signal to your brain that you're entering a situation that you're prepared for, which reduces anxiety.

**Elements of a Good Pre-Interview Routine:**

- Breathing exercises or meditation to calm nerves.
- Reviewing your key talking points and value proposition.
- Listening to uplifting music or positive affirmations.
- Visualising a successful interview.

A consistent pre-interview routine creates a mental and emotional buffer that protects you from last-minute jitters.

**Example:** Before each interview, you might spend five minutes practising deep breathing, then review your top three strengths and repeat a positive affirmation like, "I am fully prepared, and I will excel in this interview."

## Conclusion

Anxiety before and during interviews is natural, but it doesn't have to control your performance. By incorporating mindset techniques like reframing anxiety, practising visualisation, using breathing exercises, and engaging in positive self-talk, you can take control of your nerves and approach interviews with calm, confidence, and focus. Building a strong mindset not only helps you perform better in interviews but also boosts your overall sense of self-assurance in your professional life.

## Body Language: Non-Verbal Cues to Look Confident

In an interview, your body language can convey as much, if not more, than your words. Non-verbal communication plays a critical role in how you are perceived by interviewers. It reflects your confidence, professionalism, and comfort level in the interaction. Mastering confident body language ensures that your non-verbal cues align with the strong, capable impression you want to create.

Let's explore the most important aspects of body language to help you project confidence during an interview.

### 1. Maintain Good Posture: The Foundation of Confidence

Your posture speaks volumes about your self-assurance and mindset. A strong, open posture conveys that you are confident, poised, and in control. Slouching or leaning too far forward can suggest nervousness or a lack of enthusiasm, while sitting too rigidly may come off as overly tense or uncomfortable.

**How to Sit Confidently:**

- **Sit Up Straight:** Keep your back straight, shoulders slightly back, and chest open. This posture not only projects confidence but also helps you breathe easily, which supports calmness.

- **Feet Flat on the Floor:** Keeping your feet firmly planted on the ground creates a stable, grounded feeling and prevents you from fidgeting or shifting nervously in your seat.

- **Avoid Slumping or Leaning Back:** Slouching can make you appear disinterested or disengaged, while leaning too far back may come across as overly casual or arrogant. Aim for a balanced, neutral posture that shows attentiveness and professionalism.

**Example:** When you walk into the interview room, greet the interviewer with a firm handshake and maintain an upright posture as you sit down. This creates an immediate impression of confidence and readiness.

### 2. Make Eye Contact: The Window to Engagement

Eye contact is one of the most powerful non-verbal signals in an interview. It indicates that you are paying attention, engaged, and confident in your interactions.

Failing to maintain eye contact can be interpreted as disinterest, insecurity, or even dishonesty. On the other hand, staring too intensely can make the interaction uncomfortable.

**How to Make Effective Eye Contact:**

- **Engage, Don't Stare:** Make eye contact when listening to the interviewer's questions and when delivering your responses. Aim to maintain eye contact for 70-80% of the conversation, breaking it occasionally to avoid appearing too intense.

- **Use Soft Focus:** Avoid focusing too sharply on the interviewer's eyes alone. Instead, look at their face more generally to create a natural and relaxed connection.

- **Switch Between Interviewers:** If you're speaking to more than one interviewer, make sure to divide your attention and eye contact evenly between them.

**Example:** When asked a question, look the interviewer in the eye as you respond, nodding occasionally to show that you're engaged in the conversation. If there are multiple interviewers, periodically shift your eye contact to include each person, ensuring everyone feels involved.

### 3. Use Hand Gestures Thoughtfully

Hand gestures can add emphasis to your words and help communicate your ideas more effectively. However, uncontrolled or excessive hand movements can be distracting. The goal is to use natural, purposeful gestures that enhance your points and demonstrate confidence.

**How to Use Hand Gestures Effectively:**

- **Keep Movements Controlled:** Use smooth, deliberate gestures to emphasise key points, but avoid exaggerated or jerky movements that can seem nervous.

- **Rest Hands Naturally:** When you're not gesturing, keep your hands relaxed either on the table or in your lap. Avoid crossing your arms (which can seem defensive) or fidgeting with objects like pens or your clothes.

- **Match Gestures to Your Words:** Use hand movements to support what you're saying. For instance, when discussing a list of points, you can raise your fingers to count each point, or spread your hands slightly when talking about something expansive.

**Example:** When explaining a project you worked on, you might use a small, open-handed gesture to indicate collaboration with others. This makes your explanation more dynamic and engaging.

**4. Smile: Project Warmth and Positivity**

A genuine smile conveys warmth, approachability, and confidence. It helps build rapport with the interviewer, making you seem more likeable and creating a positive emotional connection. Smiling also helps you relax, which reduces nervous tension and makes you feel more at ease during the interview.

**When and How to Smile:**

- **Start with a Smile:** When you first meet the interviewer, greet them with a friendly smile to establish a positive tone from the outset.

- **Smile Naturally During the Conversation:** Smile occasionally throughout the interview, especially when discussing your achievements, strengths, or any positive aspect of your experience.

- **Balance with Seriousness:** While smiling is important, it's equally crucial to balance it with a professional demeanour. Be mindful of the context, and avoid smiling too much during serious or sensitive discussions.

**Example:** When the interviewer asks about your strengths or accomplishments, smile as you discuss your experiences. This shows that you're confident in your abilities and take pride in your work.

### 5. Mirror the Interviewer's Body Language

Subtle mirroring of the interviewer's body language can help create rapport and demonstrate that you're engaged in the conversation. Mirroring involves adopting similar postures, gestures, or energy levels as the interviewer, which subconsciously signals that you are in sync with them.

**How to Mirror Body Language Effectively:**

- **Be Subtle:** Don't directly mimic every movement or gesture the interviewer makes. Instead, adopt similar postures or gestures naturally. For example, if the interviewer leans slightly forward when asking a question, you might do the same when answering.

- **Match Their Tone and Energy:** If the interviewer speaks in a calm, measured tone, respond in kind. If they are more energetic and animated, reflect that energy in your responses and gestures.

**Example:** If the interviewer crosses their legs or rests their hands on the table while listening, you can subtly mirror their posture by doing something similar. This creates a sense of harmony and mutual respect.

### 6. Use the Power of the Pause

Confident candidates are not afraid of brief pauses during the interview. Pausing before answering a question, or after delivering an important point, gives you time to collect your thoughts and shows that you're thoughtful and composed.

**How to Use Pauses Confidently:**

- **Pause Before Answering Difficult Questions:** If you're asked a challenging question, take a deep breath and pause for a moment before responding. This not only gives you time to structure your answer but also conveys that you're thoughtful and not rushing to give a generic response.

- **Pause After Important Points:** After delivering a key point, pause briefly to let your words sink in. This gives the interviewer time to process your message and shows that you're confident in the strength of your answer.

**Example:** If the interviewer asks, "Can you tell us about a time you faced a major challenge at work?" take a second to collect your thoughts before responding. This signals that you are considering your answer carefully and aren't nervous about a few moments of silence.

### 7. Control Nervous Tics and Fidgeting

Fidgeting can be a clear sign of anxiety or nervousness, which can undermine the confident image you want to project. Common nervous habits include tapping your foot, playing with your hair, adjusting your clothing, or touching your face.

Being aware of these habits and practising calm, controlled movements can help you appear more composed.

**How to Avoid Nervous Tics:**

- **Keep Your Hands Occupied:** Rest your hands calmly on the table or in your lap. If you're tempted to fidget, gently press your fingertips together or hold a pen without clicking it.

- **Stay Mindful of Movements:** Pay attention to your body language and notice any habits that may signal nervousness. If you catch yourself fidgeting, calmly bring your hands back to a neutral position and take a deep breath to regain composure.

**Example:** If you find yourself tapping your foot under the table during the interview, place both feet flat on the floor and take a moment to steady yourself. Maintaining stillness can help convey confidence.

### Conclusion

Mastering confident body language in an interview is about being mindful of the non-verbal signals you send. Good posture, strong eye contact, thoughtful hand gestures, and a calm, controlled presence can significantly enhance the impression you make. By paying attention to these non-verbal cues, you will project confidence, professionalism, and readiness, all of which contribute to a successful interview.

### How to Develop a Confident Communication Style

A confident communication style in an interview setting is essential to making a strong, lasting impression. It's not just what you say, but how you say it that matters. Developing a communication style that radiates confidence will help you build rapport with the interviewer, articulate your strengths effectively, and demonstrate that you're the right fit for the role.

Here are several strategies for cultivating a confident communication style during interviews:

**1. Speak with Clarity and Purpose**

One of the hallmarks of confident communication is speaking clearly and with intention. Candidates who mumble, rush through their responses, or use unclear language can leave interviewers uncertain about their qualifications or unsure of their engagement. Speaking clearly ensures your key points are understood and leaves a strong impression.

**How to Improve Clarity:**

- **Slow Down:** When nervous, many people tend to speak quickly. Consciously slow your speech to ensure you articulate each word and allow the interviewer to fully absorb your points.

- **Enunciate:** Pronounce your words distinctly, avoiding any mumbling or trailing off at the end of sentences. This shows that you are deliberate in your speech and confident in your message.

- **Avoid Filler Words:** Words like "um," "like," "you know," and "sort of" can weaken your message and make you seem uncertain. Practice speaking without relying on fillers to convey more authority and confidence.

**Example:** Instead of saying, "I'm sort of responsible for managing a team, um, you know, in a way," a clearer, more confident statement would be, "I lead a team of five, overseeing project timelines and ensuring smooth collaboration."

## 2. Use a Strong, Measured Tone of Voice

Your tone of voice plays a key role in how your message is received. A weak, hesitant tone can make you appear unsure, while a loud or overly assertive tone may seem abrasive. Striking the right balance ensures you come across as confident and composed.

**Tips for Using an Authoritative Tone:**

- **Project Your Voice:** Speak at a volume that is appropriate for the room and the setting. A voice that's too quiet can signal insecurity, while a well-projected voice demonstrates confidence and control.

- **Maintain a Steady Pace:** Speaking too quickly can make you sound anxious, while speaking too slowly might come across as lacking enthusiasm. Aim for a steady, measured pace that allows you to communicate clearly without rushing.

- **Vary Your Tone for Emphasis:** A flat, monotone voice can make you sound disengaged or robotic. Use inflection to emphasise key points and add energy to your delivery, which shows that you're passionate about what you're saying.

**Example:** When describing your achievements, your tone should rise slightly to convey enthusiasm. For instance, when discussing a challenging project, you successfully led, allow your voice to reflect pride in your accomplishment.

## 3. Craft Concise and Focused Responses

Confident communicators are concise. Rambling or going off on tangents can dilute your message and make you appear unorganised.

Structured, focused answers ensure that you provide all necessary information without overwhelming or confusing the interviewer.

**Strategies for Being Concise:**

- **Answer Directly:** Listen to the interviewer's question carefully and answer it directly before offering additional details. This shows that you're thoughtful and focused on providing relevant information.

- **Use the STAR Method:** The STAR (Situation, Task, Action, Result) method is a great way to keep your responses organised and to the point. It ensures that your answers are structured and concise while clearly outlining your accomplishments.

- **Avoid Unnecessary Details:** Stick to the most important points that answer the question or demonstrate your value. Avoid veering off into unrelated anecdotes or overloading the interviewer with minor details.

**Example:** If asked, "Can you tell me about a time you solved a problem at work?" avoid launching into a long winded explanation. Instead, give a structured response using STAR: "In my previous role, we faced a challenge when a major client's project fell behind schedule (Situation). I was tasked with reorganising the workflow to meet the deadline (Task). I implemented a new tracking system and coordinated additional resources (Action), which resulted in the project being delivered on time, and we retained the client (Result)."

### 4. Ask Thoughtful Questions

Confident communicators don't just wait for their turn to speak they actively engage in the conversation.

Asking thoughtful questions demonstrates that you are engaged, curious, and well prepared. It also shows that you're confident enough to direct parts of the conversation and explore areas of interest.

**How to Ask Strong Questions:**

- **Prepare in Advance:** Research the company and role thoroughly before the interview and come prepared with insightful questions. Asking specific questions about the company's goals, culture, or challenges shows that you're genuinely interested in the role and invested in the conversation.

- **Ask Clarifying Questions:** If a question or point is unclear, don't be afraid to ask for clarification. This shows that you are listening carefully and confident enough to seek more information when necessary.

- **Inquire About Future Growth:** Asking about future opportunities, team dynamics, or how the role aligns with the company's long-term goals conveys your ambition and forward-thinking approach.

**Example:** A confident question could be, "I noticed in your recent report that the company is focusing on expanding its digital marketing efforts. How do you see this role contributing to those strategic initiatives?"

### 5. Practice Active Listening

Confident communication is a two-way street. It's not just about speaking well but also about listening attentively and responding thoughtfully. Active listening builds trust and rapport with the interviewer and ensures that your responses are tailored to what the interviewer is actually asking.

**Tips for Active Listening:**

- **Focus on the Speaker:** Maintain eye contact, nod occasionally, and give verbal cues like "I see" or "That's interesting" to show that you are engaged.

- **Don't Interrupt:** Even if you're eager to answer, wait until the interviewer has finished their question before responding. Interrupting can make you appear impatient or overly eager.

- **Reflect Back Key Points:** When appropriate, paraphrase or reflect back part of the interviewer's question before giving your answer. This not only shows that you've understood but also gives you time to craft a thoughtful response.

**Example:** If the interviewer asks, "How would you handle a conflict within your team?" you might respond, "It's important to ensure all parties feel heard and respected in a conflict situation. In my previous role..."

### 6. Use Positive, Assertive Language

The words you choose can reflect either confidence or uncertainty. Confident communicators use positive, assertive language to express their thoughts and opinions without sounding aggressive or passive.

**How to Speak Assertively:**

- **Avoid Tentative Language:** Phrases like "I think," "I'm not sure, but," or "Maybe" can undermine your authority. Replace them with more confident alternatives like "I believe," "I'm confident that," or "In my experience."

- **Own Your Achievements:** Don't downplay your accomplishments with modest language. Be proud of your successes and articulate them with certainty.

- **Use "I" Statements:** Take ownership of your contributions by using "I" statements, such as "I led the project," rather than vague or passive phrases like "the project was led by my team."

**Example:** Instead of saying, "I was kind of responsible for the team's success," say, "I led the team and played a key role in ensuring its success."

### 7. Use Pauses Strategically

Confident speakers are comfortable with short pauses in the conversation. Pausing before responding to a question or after making a key point signals that you are in control and gives your words more weight. It also allows you to gather your thoughts and avoid rushing through your answers.

**How to Use Pauses Effectively:**

- **Pause Before Answering Complex Questions:** If you're asked a particularly challenging question, don't feel pressured to jump in with an immediate answer. Take a moment to reflect, which shows that you're thoughtful and careful with your words.

- **Pause for Emphasis:** After making an important point, pause briefly to let the message sink in. This signals that you're confident in what you've said and gives the interviewer time to absorb the information.

**Example:** After describing a significant achievement, take a slight pause before continuing to your next point, allowing your statement to resonate more powerfully.

## Conclusion

Developing a confident communication style is about more than just saying the right words. It involves speaking clearly, using assertive language, listening actively, and structuring your responses with purpose. By practising these techniques, you can convey self-assurance and competence, ensuring that your interview performance leaves a lasting, positive impression on potential employers.

## Chapter 3: The First Impression

### Crafting the Perfect Introduction: The "Elevator Pitch"

Your first impression in an interview is critical, and one of the most effective tools to make that impression is a well-crafted elevator pitch. An elevator pitch is a concise, compelling introduction that summarises who you are, what you do, and why you are the right candidate all within the time it would take for a brief elevator ride, typically 30-60 seconds.

This initial statement sets the tone for the rest of the interview, capturing the interviewer's attention and providing a clear snapshot of your strengths and aspirations.

Here's how you can craft a powerful elevator pitch to make a great first impression.

### 1. Understand the Purpose of an Elevator Pitch

Your elevator pitch is not just a rote summary of your CV; it's an opportunity to sell yourself in a succinct, impactful way. It serves several purposes:

- **Introduce Yourself Clearly:** It provides the interviewer with a quick overview of who you are and what you bring to the table.

- **Highlight Your Key Strengths:** The pitch allows you to draw attention to the skills, experiences, or achievements that make you uniquely qualified for the role.
- **Engage the Interviewer:** A well-delivered elevator pitch grabs the interviewer's interest and sets the tone for a productive conversation.

Think of your pitch as a trailer for a movie: it should be engaging, concise, and make the interviewer want to know more about you.

## 2. Structure Your Elevator Pitch

A strong elevator pitch has a clear and logical structure, covering the most important aspects of your professional identity. A simple and effective structure includes:

- **Who You Are:** Start by introducing yourself with your name and your current professional role or title.
- **What You Do:** Highlight your primary expertise or your most recent role, including key responsibilities or achievements.
- **Why You're Here:** Briefly explain why you are interested in this specific role or how your skills align with the company's needs.

This structure ensures that your pitch is focused and relevant while giving the interviewer a well-rounded view of your candidacy.

**Example Structure:**

- **Who You Are:** "My name is Jane Smith, and I'm a digital marketing specialist with over five years of experience."

- **What You Do:** "In my current role at XYZ Company, I lead a team responsible for developing targeted campaigns that increased our client engagement by 40% over the past year."

- **Why You're Here:** "I'm excited about this opportunity because I'm passionate about applying my skills to a company with such a forward-thinking approach to digital transformation."

### 3. Tailor Your Pitch to the Role and Company

A one-size-fits-all elevator pitch won't have the same impact as a tailored, relevant introduction. Research the company and role thoroughly, and adjust your pitch to reflect why you're the ideal fit. This not only shows that you're well-prepared but also aligns your introduction with the company's specific needs and values.

**Tips for Tailoring Your Pitch:**

- **Align with the Company's Goals:** If the company is focused on innovation, highlight how your background in creative problem-solving or your experience with new technologies makes you a strong candidate.

- **Focus on Relevant Skills:** If the role requires particular skills, make sure your pitch mentions those. For example, if the job requires leadership, mention your experience managing teams.

- **Reflect the Company Culture:** If the company values teamwork and collaboration, subtly emphasise your ability to work well with others or lead cross-functional projects.

**Example:** If you're applying for a role at a start-up known for its fast-paced, dynamic environment, you might adjust your pitch to say: "I thrive in fast-moving environments where I can drive growth through innovative strategies, and that's what excites me about joining your team."

### 4. Highlight Your Value Proposition

Your elevator pitch is your opportunity to communicate your value proposition the unique combination of skills, experiences, and strengths you bring to the role. In a short time, you need to make it clear why hiring you will benefit the company.

**How to Showcase Your Value:**

- **Quantify Achievements:** Wherever possible, use metrics to demonstrate the impact you've had in previous roles. Numbers provide tangible evidence of your success and make your pitch more memorable.

- **Focus on Outcomes:** Rather than just listing responsibilities, focus on the results you've achieved. For example, "I managed a team" becomes much more powerful when framed as "I managed a team that delivered a 30% increase in productivity."

- **Communicate Your Differentiator:** What sets you apart from other candidates? It could be a unique skill, a specific type of experience, or a personal quality that gives you an edge. Make sure this comes through in your pitch.

**Example:** "In my last role, I spearheaded a project that reduced operational costs by 15%, and I'm excited to bring that results-driven approach to your company."

### 5. Keep It Concise and Engaging

An elevator pitch should be short typically 30-60 seconds but packed with meaningful content. The key to a great pitch is conciseness: you want to deliver maximum value in minimum time without rushing or cramming in too many details.

**Strategies for Keeping It Concise:**

- **Limit to Three Key Points:** Choose the three most important points you want to highlight (e.g., your role, a major achievement, and why you're interested in the role) and focus on them.

- **Avoid Jargon:** Keep the language simple and professional. Avoid industry jargon or overly technical language unless it's crucial to the role.

- **Practice Brevity:** Write down your elevator pitch and time yourself saying it aloud. Make adjustments to ensure it flows smoothly without exceeding the time limit.

**Example:** "I'm John Doe, a project manager with a focus on streamlining operations. At my current company, I led initiatives that cut project timelines by 20%, and I'm excited about the opportunity to bring that efficiency to your team."

### 6. Practice and Refine Your Delivery

Even the best elevator pitch can fall flat if it's delivered poorly. Practice is essential to ensuring that you can deliver your pitch confidently, clearly, and naturally.

**Tips for Polishing Your Delivery:**

- **Rehearse Aloud:** Say your pitch out loud several times to get comfortable with the flow and wording. Pay attention to your tone and pacing.

- **Avoid Sounding Scripted:** While it's important to practise, don't memorise your pitch to the point where it sounds robotic. Aim for a natural, conversational tone.

- **Get Feedback:** Practise your pitch with a friend, colleague, or mentor, and ask for feedback. They can point out areas where you might need more clarity or where your delivery could be stronger.

**Example:** After practising your pitch aloud, ask a colleague to play the role of the interviewer and critique your introduction. Make adjustments based on their feedback to ensure your delivery feels genuine and confident.

### 7. Make a Lasting Impression

Your elevator pitch is often your first chance to make an impact, so it's essential to leave a strong, positive impression. Finish with a statement or question that engages the interviewer and smoothly transitions into the rest of the conversation.

**How to Close Your Pitch:**

- **Ask a Question:** Ending with a thoughtful question can invite dialogue and show that you're interested in the role. For example, "I'm very excited about this opportunity. Could you tell me more about the team I'd be working with?"

- **Express Enthusiasm:** Close with a statement of enthusiasm for the role or the company. This leaves the interviewer with a positive feeling and shows that you're genuinely interested.

**Example:** "I'm eager to bring my skills in digital marketing to your growing team. I'd love to hear more about your upcoming campaigns and how I could contribute."

## Conclusion

Crafting the perfect elevator pitch is an art that requires careful thought, structure, and practice. By clearly introducing yourself, showcasing your value proposition, and tailoring your pitch to the specific role, you can create a powerful first impression that sets you up for success in any interview.

## How to Dress for Success

The way you dress for an interview plays a vital role in making a positive first impression. Your attire not only reflects your professionalism but also signals to the interviewer that you understand the culture and expectations of the company. Dressing appropriately helps you project confidence, capability, and respect for the opportunity.

Here's a comprehensive guide on how to dress for success and ensure your outfit complements your skills and qualifications.

### 1. Understand the Company Culture

The first step to dressing for success is understanding the company's culture. Different industries and companies have different standards for what is considered appropriate interview attire. A start-up tech company may encourage business-casual or even smart-casual attire, while a financial services firm might expect a full suit and tie.

**Steps to Understand the Culture:**

- **Research the Company:** Look up the company's website, social media, or employee reviews to get a sense of their dress code. You can also check if they post team photos or videos that show what employees wear in the office.

- **Ask HR:** If you're unsure about what's appropriate, don't hesitate to ask the HR representative or recruiter about the company's dress code for interviews. They will appreciate your attention to detail, and it will ensure you're on the right track.
- **Match the Industry Norms:** If you can't find specific information about the company, rely on industry standards. For instance, finance, law, and consultancy tend to lean towards formal wear, while creative industries or tech start-ups may be more casual.

**Example:** If you're interviewing at a creative agency, a tailored blazer and smart trousers might strike the right balance between professional and modern. For a corporate role, opt for a traditional suit and tie or formal dress to align with their conservative culture.

## 2. The Power of Formal Business Attire

In most professional settings, formal business attire is a safe and respected choice. This traditional look reflects seriousness, professionalism, and respect for the occasion. Formal business attire generally includes:

- **For Men:** A suit (matching jacket and trousers), collared shirt, tie, and polished dress shoes. Dark colours like navy, charcoal, or black are often preferred for a polished, professional look.
- **For Women:** A tailored suit (either trousers or skirt), blouse or smart top, and closed-toe shoes. Conservative colours like navy, grey, or black are ideal, and accessories should be understated.

**Why Formal Works:**

- **Projecting Professionalism:** Wearing a suit shows that you take the interview seriously and respect the role.

- **Conveying Confidence:** A well fitted suit or formal outfit can enhance your posture and make you feel more confident.

- **Leaving a Positive Impression:** Interviewers are more likely to remember you positively when you're dressed in attire that reflects professionalism and preparedness.

**Example:** If you're interviewing for a role in banking or law, a dark suit with a crisp white shirt and understated accessories sends a message that you're polished and ready to step into a professional setting.

### 3. Business Casual: Striking the Balance

In many modern workplaces, particularly in creative or tech industries, business casual attire is the standard. This dress code allows for more personal expression while still maintaining a professional appearance.

**Business Casual Guidelines:**

- **For Men:** A blazer or sport coat with dress trousers or chinos, a collared shirt (with or without a tie), and loafers or smart shoes. You can opt for lighter colours like khaki or grey, especially in creative environments.

- **For Women:** A blouse or smart top with tailored trousers or a knee-length skirt. A dress with a blazer also fits well within this category. Flats or modest heels are usually appropriate.

**When to Choose Business Casual:**

- **Creative and Start Up Industries:** If you're interviewing in a creative field like marketing, design, or tech, business casual is often the preferred choice. It shows you understand the culture while still presenting yourself as professional.

- **Casual Companies:** If the company's website or social media gives off a more relaxed vibe, business casual allows you to dress smartly without being too formal.

**Example:** For a marketing position at a dynamic start-up, you might wear a blazer over a stylish shirt, paired with chinos and loafers. For women, a smart dress with a cardigan or tailored jacket would be perfect.

### 4. The Fit and Condition of Your Clothes Matter

Regardless of whether you're opting for formal or business casual attire, the fit and condition of your clothing are crucial. Even the most expensive outfit won't make a good impression if it's ill-fitting or wrinkled.

**Fit Guidelines:**

- **For Men:** Jackets should fit well at the shoulders, with sleeves that stop just above the wrist. Trousers should be hemmed properly (not dragging on the floor or too short), and shirts should be neatly tucked.

- **For Women:** Blazers and trousers should be tailored to your body shape, with no pulling or bunching. Skirts should hit at or just above the knee. Make sure that blouses or tops aren't too tight or revealing.

**Condition Tips:**

- **Clean and Pressed:** Ensure your clothes are clean, ironed, and free of wrinkles. This shows attention to detail and pride in your appearance.

- **Check for Stains or Wear:** Check for any stains, tears, or signs of wear, such as frayed hems or missing buttons. It's best to avoid anything that looks worn out or sloppy.

- **Polished Shoes:** Make sure your shoes are polished and in good condition. Scuffed or dirty shoes can detract from an otherwise polished look.

**Example:** A well fitted suit that's tailored to your proportions looks far more professional than an off-the-rack suit that's too loose or tight. Similarly, a clean, ironed blouse is always better than one that's rumpled or stained.

### 5. Choose Neutral Colours and Simple Patterns

When it comes to interview attire, neutral colours and simple patterns are often the safest choice. Bright, flashy colours or bold patterns can be distracting and might not align with the company's culture. Sticking to classic, muted tones ensures your attire is professional and puts the focus on your qualifications.

**Recommended Colour Palette:**

- **Neutral Colours:** Navy, grey, black, white, beige, and soft pastels are typically safe and professional choices.

- **Avoid Loud Colours:** Bright reds, oranges, or neon shades can be overwhelming. If you want to introduce colour, opt for a muted tone like burgundy or forest green.

- **Simple Patterns:** Pinstripes, subtle checks, or small patterns can work well, but avoid large or busy prints.

**Example:** A navy suit with a white shirt or a grey blouse with a black skirt is timeless and professional, while a flashy red suit or floral-patterned shirt might be too distracting.

## 6. Accessorise Wisely

Accessories should complement your outfit, not dominate it. Subtlety is key when it comes to jewellery, belts, watches, and other accessories.

**Guidelines for Accessories:**

- **For Men:** A simple watch, belt, and cufflinks are usually sufficient. Avoid flashy ties or overly bold patterns.
- **For Women:** Keep jewellery minimal stud earrings, a delicate necklace, or a simple bracelet are all appropriate. Avoid large, distracting pieces.
- **Professional Bags:** If you're bringing a bag, opt for a professional briefcase or handbag. A polished leather bag looks much more professional than a casual backpack or oversized tote.

**Example:** A man might wear a classic silver watch and a solid tie, while a woman might opt for a small pendant necklace and stud earrings to complete her look without overpowering it.

## 7. Grooming and Personal Hygiene

Your personal grooming and hygiene are just as important as your outfit. Neat grooming shows respect for the interview process and indicates that you care about presenting your best self.

**Grooming Tips:**

- **Hair:** Make sure your hair is clean, neatly styled, and appropriate for the environment. If you have facial hair, it should be well-groomed.

- **Nails:** Keep your nails clean and neatly trimmed. Avoid overly bold nail polish colours.

- **Fragrance:** If you choose to wear perfume or cologne, use it sparingly. Strong fragrances can be overpowering and may cause discomfort for the interviewer.

**Example:** Neatly styled hair, a clean shave or well-groomed beard, and minimal fragrance all contribute to a polished, professional appearance.

### Conclusion

Dressing for success is about more than just following a dress code; it's about understanding the company's culture, selecting an outfit that reflects professionalism, and ensuring that every detail from the fit of your clothing to your grooming is carefully considered. By dressing appropriately and with confidence, you'll create a positive first impression that complements your skills and qualifications, setting the stage for a successful interview.

### Creating Rapport with Interviewers

Building rapport with your interviewer is one of the most effective ways to set yourself apart as a candidate. Establishing a personal connection can make the interview feel less like an interrogation and more like a conversation, helping both you and the interviewer feel comfortable. This rapport can foster trust, allow your personality to shine through, and leave a lasting, positive impression.

Here are key strategies to help you create rapport with interviewers during your next job interview.

### 1. Start with a Warm Greeting

First impressions matter, and the way you greet your interviewer sets the tone for the rest of the conversation. A warm, friendly greeting demonstrates that you are approachable, confident, and enthusiastic about the opportunity.

### Tips for a Good Greeting:

- **Smile:** A genuine smile helps to break the ice and conveys positivity. It can instantly make you seem more likeable and approachable.

- **Make Eye Contact:** Eye contact shows confidence and helps establish a connection. It signals that you're engaged and ready for the conversation.

- **Offer a Firm Handshake:** If appropriate, a firm handshake (but not too strong) is a classic professional gesture that reflects confidence. In more casual or remote settings, a nod or a verbal greeting can be equally effective.

- **Introduce Yourself Clearly:** While the interviewer may already know who you are, introducing yourself confidently shows professionalism. "Good morning, I'm [Your Name]. It's a pleasure to meet you and I'm really excited to be here today."

**Example:** Upon meeting the interviewer, smile and say, "Good morning, I'm John Smith. Thank you for taking the time to meet with me today I'm really looking forward to our conversation."

## 2. Find Common Ground

One of the easiest ways to create rapport is to find common ground. This might involve something as simple as commenting on the weather or talking about a shared professional interest. Finding these small points of connection can help break the ice and establish a more comfortable environment.

**Strategies for Finding Common Ground:**

- **Research the Interviewer:** Before the interview, do some research on the interviewer's professional background. If they have written articles or participated in relevant events, briefly mention it. For example, "I noticed that you gave a talk on leadership at the recent industry conference. I found it very insightful."

- **Comment on the Surroundings:** If the interview is in-person, making an observation about the office environment or the company's culture can be an easy conversation starter.

- **Relate to Shared Experiences:** If you know that the interviewer has a similar career path or background, subtly weave that into the conversation. This could be shared experience in a particular industry, similar education, or working for the same type of organisation.

**Example:** "I see that you started your career in healthcare project management similar to my background. It's always inspiring to connect with others who've had experience in that space."

## 3. Show Genuine Interest in the Interviewer

Building rapport isn't just about making yourself likeable it's also about showing that you're interested in the person you're talking to.

Asking thoughtful questions about the interviewer's role or their experiences with the company can foster connection and demonstrate your curiosity.

**How to Show Interest:**

- **Ask About Their Experience:** During the interview, you might ask the interviewer about their own career path or how they've found working at the company. This personalises the interaction and can make the conversation more engaging.

- **Listen Actively:** When the interviewer talks about the company or their own experiences, listen carefully. Nod, smile, or make verbal acknowledgements ("That's interesting," or "I'd love to hear more about that") to show that you're genuinely engaged.

- **Use Follow-Up Questions:** If the interviewer mentions something particularly interesting or relevant, follow up with a brief question. This keeps the conversation flowing and shows that you're paying attention.

**Example:** "I'd love to hear more about your journey with the company. What do you enjoy most about your role here?"

### 4. Mirror Their Communication Style

Mirroring is a subtle psychological technique where you reflect the body language, tone, and energy of the person you're speaking with. When used naturally, it helps create a sense of harmony and alignment, making the interviewer feel more comfortable and connected with you.

**Ways to Mirror Effectively:**

- **Match Their Energy Level:** If the interviewer is more formal and reserved, maintain a similar professional tone. If they're more casual and conversational, feel free to relax your tone slightly (while staying professional). This helps to create a balanced, comfortable dialogue.

- **Use Similar Body Language:** Without mimicking, you can align your posture or gestures with those of the interviewer. For instance, if they're sitting back in their chair, you might also adopt a more relaxed posture. If they're leaning forward and animated, you can subtly reflect that energy.

- **Adjust Your Speaking Pace:** If the interviewer speaks quickly and with a lot of energy, try to match that pace. Similarly, if they're more measured in their speaking, adjust your tone and speed to complement theirs.

**Example:** If the interviewer is relaxed and conversational, you might lean slightly forward and use a more casual tone while still maintaining professionalism. If they're more formal, keep your posture upright and your tone serious.

### 5. Be Empathetic and Authentic

While building rapport, it's crucial to remain authentic and not overdo it. Trying too hard to please or impress can come off as insincere. Instead, focus on being genuine and empathetic in your responses, ensuring that you are presenting your real self.

**How to Stay Authentic:**

- **Be Yourself:** Don't feel the need to adopt a personality that doesn't align with who you are. Being authentic helps to create a more genuine connection.

- **Acknowledge the Interviewer's Point of View:** Show empathy when the interviewer discusses challenges or important aspects of the role. For example, if they mention a current challenge in the company, you can express understanding and offer your thoughts on how you might help.
- **Share Real Stories:** When answering questions, share personal experiences that reflect who you are. This authenticity makes you more relatable and memorable.

**Example:** If the interviewer talks about the challenges the team is facing, you might respond with, "I completely understand how that could be difficult. In my last role, we faced a similar challenge, and what really helped was [insert solution]."

### 6. Use Positive Language and Stay Engaged

Positivity goes a long way in building rapport. Using upbeat, confident language makes you more likeable and keeps the conversation flowing smoothly. Staying engaged and showing enthusiasm for the role and the company further strengthens the connection between you and the interviewer.

**Tips for Positive Engagement:**

- **Use Positive Body Language:** Nod occasionally, smile when appropriate, and maintain good posture to show that you're fully engaged in the conversation.
- **Stay Enthusiastic:** Let your interest in the position and company come through in your tone and language. Enthusiasm is contagious and helps to create a positive atmosphere.
- **Avoid Negative Topics:** Even if asked about a negative experience, frame your responses positively by focusing on what you learned or how you grew from the situation.

**Example:** "I'm really excited about this opportunity. From what I've read and from what you've shared, it sounds like a place where I could contribute and continue to develop my skills."

### 7. End with Gratitude and Enthusiasm

As the interview winds down, maintain the rapport you've built by ending on a positive, grateful note. Expressing appreciation for the interviewer's time and reiterating your enthusiasm for the role leaves a lasting, favourable impression.

**Effective Ways to Close:**

- **Thank the Interviewer:** Always thank the interviewer for their time and the opportunity to discuss the role. This is a small but meaningful gesture that reinforces your professionalism.

- **Reaffirm Your Interest:** Let the interviewer know that the conversation has further solidified your interest in the position.

- **End on a Friendly Note:** A simple closing remark like, "I've really enjoyed our conversation today," adds a personal touch.

**Example:** "Thank you so much for taking the time to speak with me today. This conversation has made me even more excited about the opportunity, and I look forward to the next steps."

### Conclusion

Creating rapport with interviewers is a key part of making a strong, memorable impression. By starting with a warm greeting, finding common ground, showing genuine interest, and using positive body language, you can turn the interview into a more engaging and comfortable experience for both parties.

Rapport building allows you to showcase not only your qualifications but also your interpersonal skills, making you a more attractive candidate for the role.

## Chapter 4: Handling Common Interview Questions

### The STAR Method for Behavioural Questions

One of the most important skills to master in an interview is answering behavioural questions, which typically start with prompts like "Tell me about a time when..." or "Can you give an example of...".

These questions are designed to assess how you've handled situations in the past and to predict how you might perform in the future. Employers are keen to understand your problem-solving, teamwork, and leadership abilities through these real-life examples.

A widely accepted and effective approach for answering behavioural questions is the **STAR method**. STAR stands for **Situation**, **Task**, **Action**, and **Result**. This structured response format allows you to clearly and concisely explain the context of your story, the specific challenge, the steps you took, and the outcome, ensuring your answer is complete and focused.

### 1. Situation: Setting the Scene

The first step in the STAR method is to describe the **Situation**. This involves providing context to the scenario or event you're referring to. It's important to be brief but detailed enough for the interviewer to understand the background of the story.

When you're setting up the situation, focus on what is relevant to the interviewer and the job you're applying for. Avoid unnecessary details, but make sure the context is clear.

Keep the following in mind:

- What was the specific scenario you were dealing with?
- Where did this situation occur? (e.g., workplace, team project, etc.)
- Who was involved? (e.g., coworkers, clients, managers)

**Example of Situation:** *"At my previous job as a marketing coordinator, we were preparing for the launch of a major campaign for one of our largest clients. Three weeks before the launch, we discovered that some key market data we were using was inaccurate, and we were at risk of missing the deadline."*

### 2. Task: Defining the Problem or Responsibility

After describing the situation, explain the **Task** you were assigned or the problem that needed solving. This part of the STAR method focuses on your specific role or responsibility in the scenario. This is the step where you make clear what was expected of you or the challenge you were facing.

Key points to include:

- What were your specific responsibilities in this scenario?
- What was the challenge or goal you were tasked with achieving?
- Why was it important to resolve this issue?

**Example of Task:** *"As the lead on the data analysis team, I was responsible for ensuring the accuracy of the data and making sure the campaign launch stayed on track. My job was to identify the errors in the data and correct them without delaying the project."*

## 3. Action: Explaining What You Did

This is where the bulk of your answer will be. The **Action** section is your opportunity to showcase how you approached the challenge, what steps you took, and how you applied your skills. Focus on your individual contribution, even if it was a team effort, and explain your thought process and strategy.

Key elements to cover:

- What specific actions did you take to address the task?
- What strategies or processes did you use?
- How did you involve others or lead the team?
- Were there any challenges you had to overcome along the way?

It's important to remain clear and concise when describing your actions, ensuring that each step is easy for the interviewer to follow.

**Example of Action:** *"I quickly convened a meeting with my team to go over the data discrepancies. I assigned each team member specific areas to re-analyse, while I worked directly with our data suppliers to get updated information. I also coordinated with the client to manage their expectations, keeping them informed of our progress and the changes we were making. We used real-time project management tools to ensure that every task was tracked and completed on time."*

## 4. Result: Highlighting the Outcome

The final part of the STAR method is the **Result**. This is where you demonstrate the success of your actions and show the positive outcome that came from your efforts.

Whenever possible, quantify your results (e.g., in terms of time saved, costs reduced, or customer satisfaction improved) to give the interviewer a clear picture of the impact you made.

Key points to highlight:

- What was the outcome of your efforts?
- Did you meet or exceed expectations?
- How did your actions benefit the company, the team, or the client?
- What did you learn from the experience?

**Example of Result:** *"Thanks to the team's quick action, we were able to correct the data and still launch the campaign on schedule. The client was very pleased with our transparency throughout the process, and the campaign resulted in a 15% increase in their customer engagement. Our management team praised our proactive approach and the project was considered one of the most successful launches of the year."*

**Practical Application of the STAR Method**

Mastering the STAR method involves practice, as it requires you to reflect on past experiences and express them in a structured way. When preparing for an interview, it's helpful to have multiple STAR examples in your mind. For each one, consider common competencies employers look for, such as problem-solving, teamwork, leadership, adaptability, and communication skills.

Here are some examples of behavioural questions you might encounter and how you could apply the STAR method:

1. **"Tell me about a time when you had to deal with a difficult client or customer."**
   - **Situation:** Describe the client or customer's issue.
   - **Task:** Explain your role in resolving the issue.
   - **Action:** Detail the steps you took to address their concerns.
   - **Result:** Conclude with the positive outcome, such as a satisfied customer or a renewed business relationship.

2. **"Can you give an example of a time when you worked as part of a team?"**
   - **Situation:** Set the context by describing the project or task.
   - **Task:** Define your role within the team.
   - **Action:** Discuss how you collaborated with others and the specific contributions you made.
   - **Result:** Highlight the success of the team's efforts and what was achieved as a result.

3. **"Describe a time when you faced a significant challenge at work."**
   - **Situation:** Explain the challenge you were facing.
   - **Task:** Clarify your responsibilities in overcoming this obstacle.
   - **Action:** Describe the strategic steps you took to resolve the challenge.

- **Result:** Summarise the positive impact your actions had on the situation, and mention any lessons learned.

## Conclusion

The STAR method is a powerful tool for answering behavioural interview questions in a way that is both structured and impactful. By breaking your response into clear sections (Situation, Task, Action, and Result), you ensure that your answer is organised, complete, and easy for the interviewer to follow. When used effectively, the STAR method allows you to showcase your experiences, skills, and achievements, ultimately helping you make a strong impression in the interview.

## How to Discuss Weaknesses Effectively

One of the most commonly dreaded interview questions is, "What is your greatest weakness?" It can feel like a trap, but it's actually an opportunity to demonstrate self-awareness, honesty, and a commitment to personal development. Hiring managers ask this question to see how well you understand yourself and to gauge how you handle challenges or setbacks.

The key to answering this question effectively is to approach it with transparency, while focusing on how you're actively working to overcome your weakness. Here's a structured guide on how to navigate this tricky subject:

### 1. Choose a Real, Relevant Weakness

When preparing to discuss a weakness, resist the temptation to offer a fake flaw disguised as a strength, like "I'm a perfectionist" or "I work too hard." Interviewers can usually spot these responses and might interpret them as insincere or evasive.

Instead, choose a genuine weakness that doesn't directly undermine the core requirements of the job, but is still meaningful.

For example:

- If you're applying for a management role, avoid mentioning weaknesses in leadership or communication.
- If the job requires detailed project management, don't highlight poor organisational skills.

Select a weakness that is both honest and something you've made tangible efforts to improve.

**Examples of Weaknesses:**

- Difficulty with public speaking or presenting to large groups.
- Struggling with delegating tasks and preferring to do things yourself.
- Over-commitment or taking on too much at once, leading to occasional stress.
- Being overly critical of your own work.

**Example Answer:** *"I've historically found public speaking to be quite challenging. I used to get very nervous when speaking in front of large groups, which affected my ability to communicate clearly. However, recognising that this is an essential skill, I've actively sought opportunities to improve. I've attended public speaking workshops and volunteered to present in smaller settings, which has gradually increased my confidence."*

## 2. Frame It as a Learning Opportunity

Once you've identified a real weakness, the next step is to show how you're addressing it.

The goal is to demonstrate that you're not only aware of your shortcomings but that you also take proactive steps to improve. This approach shows maturity, resilience, and a growth mindset.

Employers value candidates who can turn weaknesses into learning opportunities. When you frame your answer in this way, you show that you're adaptable and willing to evolve.

**How to Do This:**

- Explain what steps you've taken to improve or manage this weakness.

- Highlight any training, courses, or personal initiatives you've undertaken to develop this area.

- Share any progress or specific instances where you've overcome the weakness.

**Example Answer:** *"Delegating tasks has been something I've struggled with, as I tend to want to take on projects myself to ensure everything is done to my standards. However, I've learned that this approach isn't sustainable in leadership roles, so I've started to consciously delegate more. I now prioritise training my team members and trusting them to complete tasks, which has not only improved team efficiency but also developed their skills."*

### 3. Connect it Back to the Job and Your Strengths

A great way to finish your response is by bringing the discussion back to the role and highlighting how your actions to improve your weakness benefit the job you're applying for. You can also briefly touch on how the same challenge has honed other strengths, ensuring that the focus isn't entirely negative.

By positioning your weakness in a positive light and connecting it to your potential contributions to the company, you demonstrate that you've learned valuable lessons that will make you a stronger employee.

**How to Link Back to the Job:**

- Explain how the skills or techniques you've developed to overcome the weakness will benefit you in the new role.

- Highlight any strengths that you've developed as a result of tackling your weakness.

**Example Answer:** *"In terms of my struggle with public speaking, I've grown significantly more confident, and I'm now able to deliver presentations and communicate ideas more clearly. This has proven to be invaluable in team meetings and client interactions.*

*I feel this continued development will benefit me in this role, as effective communication is critical when leading projects or presenting reports."*

### 4. Avoid Overly Critical Weaknesses or Clichés

While honesty is key, there are certain weaknesses that can be detrimental to your application if not handled carefully. Avoid mentioning weaknesses that could raise red flags about your ability to perform in the role. For instance, if you're applying for a customer facing role, don't admit to being impatient with clients or struggling with communication.

Additionally, steer clear of clichéd responses like "I care too much" or "I'm a workaholic" they tend to come across as insincere or self-serving.

**Common Pitfalls to Avoid:**

- Don't mention a weakness that is critical to the role, like poor time management for a project manager position.

- Avoid framing strengths as weaknesses. This tactic has been overused and can come off as disingenuous.

- Don't dwell too long on the negative aspects of your weakness. Quickly move on to how you're addressing it.

**Examples of Weaknesses to Avoid for Certain Roles:**

- **For a management role:** Mentioning difficulty with leadership or decision making could be problematic.

- **For a sales role:** Saying you're not comfortable with cold-calling or rejection.

- **For a technical role:** Admitting to a lack of attention to detail or poor technical skills.

### 5. Practice Delivering Your Response

Like any interview answer, your response to the "weakness" question should be well-rehearsed but not robotic. Practising beforehand allows you to speak confidently, avoid rambling, and strike the right tone one that acknowledges the weakness without being overly self-critical.

Here are some final tips:

- **Be concise:** Keep your answer brief and to the point, usually around 1-2 minutes.

- **Stay positive:** Focus on growth and improvement rather than dwelling on the weakness itself.

- **Be honest but strategic:** Choose a weakness that is honest but not damaging to your candidacy.

**Sample Answer:**

**Example 1 (For a Project Manager Role):** *"One area I've been working on is learning to delegate more effectively. Earlier in my career, I had a tendency to take on too much responsibility myself, as I wanted to ensure every detail was perfect. However, I've come to realise that effective project management requires trusting your team and allowing them to take ownership of tasks. Over the past year, I've consciously worked on delegating more and mentoring my team members, which has improved overall project efficiency and strengthened team morale."*

**Example 2 (For a Customer Service Role):** *"In the past, I've found it challenging to handle difficult customers without getting personally affected. I would sometimes let negative interactions impact my mood. However, I've worked hard to improve my emotional resilience by focusing on active listening and empathy, as well as separating personal feelings from professional interactions.*

*I now take a step back after each challenging conversation and review how I can improve next time. This has significantly reduced my stress levels and allowed me to provide better customer service."*

## Conclusion

Answering the weakness question effectively requires a balance of honesty, self-awareness, and a focus on growth. By choosing a relevant but manageable weakness, framing it as an area for development, and discussing how you're actively working to improve, you can turn a challenging question into an opportunity to showcase your personal growth and commitment to continuous improvement.

Remember to keep your response positive and forward looking, ensuring that the interviewer understands you're not defined by your weakness, but by how you respond to it.

### Answering Salary Expectation Questions Tactfully

Discussing salary expectations in an interview can be delicate, but with the right approach, it can be an opportunity to demonstrate professionalism and negotiation skills. Hiring managers ask this question to ensure your salary expectations align with their budget and to gauge how you value your skills. The key is to provide a well-considered response that shows flexibility while ensuring your compensation matches your experience and the role's responsibilities.

Here's how to answer salary expectation questions tactfully:

### 1. Research Before the Interview

Before stepping into any interview, it's crucial to have a solid understanding of the market rate for the position you're applying for. Salaries can vary significantly based on factors such as location, industry, company size, and level of experience. Doing your homework will give you a realistic range and help you avoid under- or overpricing yourself.

Here are some key steps for research:

- **Check industry-specific salary surveys** to find benchmarks for similar roles.

- Use platforms like **Glassdoor**, **PayScale**, or **LinkedIn Salary** to see what comparable roles pay in your area.

- **Network with professionals** in your field to gain insider knowledge about current salary trends.

Having this information allows you to be confident when discussing compensation, and shows the interviewer that you've done your homework.

**Example Answer (Post-Research):** *"Based on my research into similar roles in this industry and location, along with my experience and skills, I believe a salary range of £45,000 to £50,000 is appropriate for this position."*

## 2. Deflect the Question (If Asked Too Early)

If the salary expectation question arises early in the interview, it's best to delay providing a specific figure. This is because at the initial stage, you may not yet have a full understanding of the role's scope, responsibilities, and potential benefits package. Deflecting the question tactfully can buy you time to gather more information.

Strategies to delay:

- Politely express your interest in learning more about the position before discussing salary.
- Ask about the company's budget or range for the role.

**Example Answer:** *"I'd love to understand more about the full scope of the role and responsibilities before discussing specific salary expectations. Could you tell me more about the range the company has in mind for this position?"*

Alternatively: *"At this point, I'm focused on finding the right role and company where I can add value. I'd be happy to discuss salary once we've covered the details of the job and responsibilities."*

This type of response signals your willingness to discuss salary at the appropriate time while emphasising your interest in the role itself rather than just the compensation.

### 3. Offer a Range, Not a Specific Figure

When you are ready to discuss salary expectations, it's best to provide a range rather than a fixed number. Offering a range allows room for negotiation and signals flexibility to the employer, while still conveying your expectations. Ensure the lower end of your range is something you'd be comfortable with, and that the top end is aspirational but realistic.

The range you provide should be based on your research and take into account your experience, skills, and market conditions. Keep in mind any non-monetary benefits or perks the company offers, such as remote work options, health benefits, or extra holiday time, which may influence your desired salary.

**Example Answer:** *"Based on my experience and the research I've done on market salaries for this role, I believe a range of £55,000 to £60,000 would be appropriate. However, I'm open to discussing this further based on the overall compensation package."*

By offering a range, you signal that you're open to negotiation, which is often appreciated by hiring managers.

### 4. Highlight Your Value Proposition

When discussing salary expectations, it's essential to remind the interviewer of the unique value you bring to the table. Salary discussions aren't just about the company's budget; they're also about justifying your compensation based on the skills, experience, and impact you'll have on the organisation.

Before naming a salary range, briefly touch on your qualifications and contributions you could make to the company. This frames the conversation as being about the value you bring, not just the salary you want.

**Example Answer:** *"Given my five years of experience in managing successful marketing campaigns, along with my expertise in digital marketing strategy, I'm confident that I can make a strong contribution to your team. Based on market research and my skills, I believe a salary in the range of £50,000 to £55,000 would be appropriate."*

This approach allows you to remind the employer why you're worth what you're asking for.

### 5. Express Flexibility

It's important to show flexibility during salary discussions. While you should know your worth, being rigid can sometimes come across as a red flag to employers. Expressing a willingness to negotiate can make the conversation smoother and leave room for discussion around bonuses, benefits, or potential raises in the future.

**How to Show Flexibility:**

- Mention that salary is only one aspect of the total package.
- Indicate your openness to negotiate based on the full compensation structure, which could include health benefits, bonuses, stock options, or learning and development opportunities.

**Example Answer:** *"While salary is important, I'm also very interested in the overall opportunity with the company, including the culture and professional growth it offers. I'm open to discussing compensation further to ensure we find a mutually beneficial arrangement."*

This kind of response reassures the employer that while you have salary expectations, you're also focused on the broader picture of what the role can offer.

## 6. When You're Asked to Provide Your Current Salary

Some interviewers may ask about your current salary. In certain countries and regions, this question is no longer permitted by law, but in places where it is still legal, it's crucial to navigate it tactfully. You don't want to undersell yourself if you're currently earning below market value, but you also want to maintain transparency.

One way to respond is to redirect the focus back to the market rate and the role at hand, rather than your past earnings.

**Example Answer:** *"My current salary is £40,000, but I believe that my experience and the responsibilities of this new role would justify compensation more in line with market rates, which I understand to be between £45,000 and £50,000."*

This way, you're being honest about your current salary but positioning the conversation around your value in the context of the new role.

## 7. Handling Lowball Offers

If the salary offer you receive is significantly below your expectations, it's important to handle this situation diplomatically. Start by expressing gratitude for the offer and reassert your enthusiasm for the role, then tactfully explain that the salary doesn't align with your expectations based on your experience and the market rate.

You can use this as an opportunity to negotiate and potentially improve the offer by discussing other benefits or perks.

**Example Answer:** *"Thank you so much for the offer I'm really excited about the role and working with your team. Based on my experience and research into comparable positions, I was expecting a salary more in the range of £50,000 to £55,000.*

*Is there flexibility in the offer, or perhaps additional benefits we could discuss to bridge the gap?"*

By phrasing it this way, you maintain a positive tone while clearly communicating that the offer doesn't meet your expectations.

### Conclusion

Answering salary expectation questions tactfully is all about preparation, flexibility, and focusing on your value. By researching ahead of time, framing the conversation around your skills and contributions, and showing openness to negotiation, you can navigate this tricky question with confidence. Keep the conversation professional and positive, and always aim to find a mutually beneficial outcome that aligns with your experience and the role's demands.

### Chapter 5: Asking the Right Questions

### Why You Should Ask Questions as an Interviewee

One of the most crucial yet often overlooked parts of an interview is the opportunity for candidates to ask their own questions. When the interviewer says, "Do you have any questions for us?" it is not merely a formality. This is your chance to gather valuable insights into the company and role, and it's also a moment for you to demonstrate deeper engagement with the opportunity at hand.

The questions you ask can shape the interviewer's perception of you. Not only do they show that you've done your research, but they also highlight your level of critical thinking, curiosity, and desire to ensure the role is the right fit for you.

Here's why asking thoughtful questions as an interviewee is vital:

### 1. Shows Interest and Enthusiasm

When you ask insightful, well researched questions, it signals that you are genuinely interested in the role and the organisation. Employers want to hire people who are excited about the job, and asking questions proves that you're not just passively going through the motions you're actively engaged.

Good questions convey that:

- You've researched the company and are curious about how it operates.

- You're thinking about how you can contribute to the team.

- You want to understand the company's culture, goals, and challenges.

**Example Questions:**

- *"I noticed your company recently expanded into new markets. How do you see this role supporting that growth in the next year?"*

- *"Can you tell me more about the company culture and how teams typically collaborate across departments?"*

By showing a deep interest, you can leave a lasting impression on your interviewer, increasing your chances of standing out from other candidates.

### 2. Helps You Assess Company Fit

Interviews are not just for the employer to evaluate you it's also your opportunity to evaluate them. You are assessing whether this company and role align with your values, work style, and career goals.

Asking the right questions helps you get a clearer picture of the company's culture, work environment, management style, and future outlook.

**Key Areas to Assess Through Questions:**

- **Work-Life Balance:** Is the company's approach to work-life balance compatible with your personal needs?
- **Team Dynamics:** How do teams communicate and collaborate? Do you prefer the leadership style they promote?
- **Growth Opportunities:** Does the company offer opportunities for learning and career advancement?
- **Job Expectations:** Is the role's scope aligned with your skills and ambitions?

**Example Questions:**

- "Can you describe what a typical day in this role looks like?"
- "How does the company support professional development and career growth?"
- "What are the biggest challenges the team is facing right now, and how would this role help address them?"

These questions help you gauge whether this is the right environment for you and if it's a place where you can thrive.

**3. Clarifies Job Expectations and Success Metrics**

Even if a job description looks appealing, there can be nuances in every role that aren't immediately apparent. Asking questions can help you get a clear understanding of what success looks like in this role and how your performance will be evaluated. It's important to understand the expectations upfront so that you can assess if they align with your skills and professional goals.

**Questions That Clarify Role Expectations:**

- *"How do you define success in this role during the first six months?"*
- *"What are the key challenges someone in this position might face?"*
- *"How is performance evaluated, and what does career progression look like for someone in this role?"*

By asking these questions, you'll gain a clearer picture of the day-to-day responsibilities and the company's priorities, ensuring there are no surprises after you join.

## 4. Demonstrates Critical Thinking and Strategic Insight

Employers appreciate candidates who demonstrate the ability to think critically and strategically. The questions you ask can reflect how well you've analysed the company, the market, and the potential challenges the business may face. This is a chance to show that you're already thinking about how you can add value to the organisation.

For example, asking about future challenges or business strategies shows that you're not just focused on getting hired but are already thinking like a future employee.

**Strategic Questions to Ask:**

- *"What are the key challenges you see this department facing over the next year, and how can this role help overcome them?"*
- *"How does this role contribute to the company's broader goals and long-term vision?"*

These types of questions can set you apart by showing the interviewer that you have a proactive and strategic mindset.

You're not only thinking about your own career but also about how you can contribute to the company's success.

## 5. Builds Rapport with the Interviewer

Asking thoughtful, engaging questions fosters a more natural conversation with the interviewer, helping to build rapport and establish a connection. People hire individuals they feel comfortable with, and when the interview feels like a two-way dialogue, it makes the experience more memorable for both parties.

By asking questions that are tailored to the individual interviewer's role or experience, you can also gain valuable insights that go beyond the job description.

**Questions That Build Rapport:**

- *"What do you enjoy most about working for this company?"*
- *"How long have you been with the company, and what's kept you motivated here?"*
- *"What's the most exciting project or initiative you're currently working on?"*

These questions encourage the interviewer to share their own experiences, helping you develop a more personal connection with them. This rapport building can work in your favour when final decisions are being made.

## 6. Uncovers Red Flags

Not all companies are a good fit for every candidate, and interviews provide an important opportunity to identify potential red flags. Thoughtfully crafted questions can help reveal issues that may not have been obvious earlier in the process, such as high turnover, lack of advancement opportunities, or a toxic work environment.

**Questions That Help Identify Red Flags:**

- *"Can you tell me why the last person in this role left?"*
- *"How would you describe the management style of the leadership team?"*
- *"What's the typical path for career advancement within the company?"*

If the interviewer hesitates or gives vague answers, it could signal underlying issues within the company. This information is critical for making an informed decision about whether to accept the role if offered.

### Conclusion

Asking the right questions in an interview is essential for both gathering critical information and demonstrating your interest and value. Thoughtful questions show that you're engaged, professional, and interested in making a long-term contribution to the company. They also help you evaluate whether the position is right for you.

Remember, the best interviews are two-way conversations. By preparing intelligent, strategic questions, you not only give yourself an edge over other candidates but also gain the insights needed to ensure the role aligns with your career goals and values.

### Examples of Insightful Questions to Ask About the Role, Company Culture, and Team Dynamics

Asking insightful questions is crucial in demonstrating your interest in the role and ensuring it's a good fit for both you and the company. The questions you ask reflect your curiosity, strategic thinking, and commitment to making informed career decisions.

Here are examples of thoughtful questions you can ask, broken down into three key areas: the role, company culture, and team dynamics.

**1. Questions About the Role**

These questions help you gain a deeper understanding of the responsibilities, expectations, and potential challenges associated with the position.

They also give insight into how success is defined and measured, allowing you to align your goals with the organisation's priorities.

- **What does success look like in this role during the first six months and beyond?**
  *This question shows you're focused on delivering value and are eager to understand the performance metrics. It also gives you a sense of what the company expects from someone in this position, especially in the short term.*

- **Can you describe a typical day or week in this role?**
  *This allows you to envision what the daily tasks and responsibilities will be and helps you assess whether this aligns with your strengths and preferences.*

- **What are the most pressing challenges the person in this role will face?**
  *Asking about challenges shows you're realistic about the position and willing to take on tough aspects. It also provides insight into any obstacles you might need to prepare for.*

- **How does this role contribute to the company's long-term goals or mission?**
  *This question demonstrates strategic thinking, as it indicates you're interested in understanding how your work will support broader organisational objectives.*

- **What are the opportunities for growth and professional development in this position?**
  *This signals your ambition and desire for career progression while also giving you insight into the company's commitment to employee development.*

### 2. Questions About Company Culture

Understanding the company culture is crucial for determining whether the environment will allow you to thrive. The following questions will help you assess whether the company's values, work style, and expectations match your preferences.

- **How would you describe the company culture, and what are the core values that guide the organisation?**
  *This provides a snapshot of the company's values and work environment, helping you assess whether they align with your own principles.*

- **How does the company support work-life balance for employees?**
  *Asking about work-life balance shows you value a healthy work environment and can uncover insights about working hours, flexibility, and overall employee satisfaction.*

- **Can you tell me about any initiatives or activities that promote team bonding and collaboration?**
  *This question helps you assess the company's efforts to build a positive work culture and the importance they place on fostering good relationships among employees.*

- **What is the company's approach to diversity, equity, and inclusion?**
  *This question signals that you care about diversity and inclusivity, and it allows you to gauge the company's commitment to fostering an equitable and supportive workplace.*

- **How has the company evolved over the past few years, and how do you see it growing in the future?**
  *This question shows that you're forward-thinking and interested in the company's long-term strategy, while also giving you insight into the stability and growth prospects of the organisation.*

## 3. Questions About Team Dynamics

Team dynamics can make or break your job satisfaction. These questions will help you understand how teams work together, the management style of your potential boss, and how the team communicates and collaborates.

- **Can you tell me about the team I'll be working with? What are their backgrounds and working styles?**
  *This helps you understand the makeup of your potential team, their expertise, and whether the team culture aligns with how you prefer to work.*

- **How does the team typically communicate and collaborate on projects?**
  *This question reveals how information is shared and how decisions are made within the team, helping you assess whether you'll fit into the communication style.*

- **What is the management style of the person I'll be reporting to?**
  *Understanding the leadership style of your direct supervisor is crucial in determining whether it aligns with how you prefer to be managed. This helps you assess if the manager will provide the guidance, autonomy, or support you need.*

- **How are conflicts or differences of opinion handled within the team?**
  *Asking this question signals emotional intelligence and a proactive approach to teamwork. It can give you insight into whether the team has a collaborative and respectful environment or whether conflicts are poorly managed.*

- **Can you tell me about a recent success the team has achieved and how they accomplished it?**
  *This question helps you understand how the team defines and celebrates success, as well as how well they work together to achieve common goals.*

### Conclusion

Asking insightful questions about the role, company culture, and team dynamics not only provides you with critical information to make an informed decision but also leaves a strong impression on the interviewer. Thoughtful, targeted questions reflect your interest in the company, show your preparedness, and help ensure that the opportunity is the right fit for your career aspirations and working style.

By digging deeper with these types of questions, you'll gain a clearer picture of what to expect in the job, how well you'll fit into the company, and whether the team environment will allow you to succeed.

**What Questions to Avoid**

While asking insightful questions is key to making a strong impression during an interview, certain types of questions can leave a negative impression on your interviewer. These are often questions that come across as self-serving, show a lack of preparation, or focus on the wrong priorities.

To ensure your questions strengthen your candidacy, avoid the following types:

## 1. Questions That Could Have Been Answered Through Basic Research

Asking questions that are easily answered by browsing the company's website, reading the job description, or reviewing recent news coverage can make you seem unprepared or uninterested. Interviewers expect you to have done your homework, so make sure your questions reflect a deeper understanding of the company and role.

**Examples to Avoid:**

- *"What does your company do?"*
  (This information should be known before the interview.)

- *"How long has the company been in business?"*
  (Such basic details are readily available on the company's website.)

**Better Approach:**
Ask questions that demonstrate you've done your research and are interested in more nuanced aspects of the company, such as recent projects, strategic changes, or challenges they're facing.

- *"I saw that the company recently expanded into new markets. How do you see this impacting the team I'd be working with?"*

## 2. Questions About Salary, Benefits, and Holidays Too Early in the Process

While it's natural to want to know about salary and benefits, bringing these up too early in the interview can give the impression that you're more interested in what you'll get from the company rather than what you can offer.

Salary discussions are often best left until later stages, once the interviewer has shown serious interest in you as a candidate.

**Examples to Avoid:**

- *"How much will I get paid?"*
- *"How many vacation days do I get?"*
- *"Do you offer bonuses or pay rises regularly?"*

**Better Approach:**
Wait until the employer signals that they're seriously considering you for the role or until the offer stage to ask about compensation and benefits. If they bring it up earlier, you can discuss it then.

- *"I'm excited about the role and the opportunity to contribute. I'd be happy to discuss compensation once we've gone over more details about the position."*

## 3. Questions That Come Across as Entitled or Self-Centred

Asking questions that solely focus on what the company can do for you, rather than what you can offer the company, can come across as entitled. While it's important to ensure the role is a good fit for you, focusing too much on perks, benefits, or your own preferences can make it seem like you're more concerned with your own interests than the organisation's needs.

**Examples to Avoid:**

- *"How soon can I get promoted?"*
- *"Can I work from home every day?"*
- *"How flexible are you with work hours and time off?"*

**Better Approach:**
Frame your questions around how you can contribute to the team and the company's goals, or ask about opportunities for growth and development without coming across as demanding or entitled.

- *"What opportunities are there for professional development in this role?"*
- *"How does the company support employees in advancing their skills and careers?"*

### 4. Questions That Are Overly Generic or Vague

Asking questions that are too broad or vague can make it seem like you haven't thought carefully about the role or company. Generic questions may not provide meaningful information, and they don't showcase your knowledge or genuine interest.

**Examples to Avoid:**

- *"Can you tell me more about the company?"*
  (This is too broad and doesn't show specific interest.)
- *"What's the work environment like?"*
  (This lacks depth and could apply to any company.)

**Better Approach:**
Ask more specific and targeted questions that reflect your understanding of the company and your interest in the specific role or team.

- *"How would you describe the company culture in terms of collaboration and innovation?"*

- *"What are the biggest challenges the team is currently facing, and how could I contribute?"*

## 5. Questions That Make You Seem Overly Concerned About Job Security

While it's important to understand the stability of the company, asking questions that focus too much on job security can signal a lack of confidence or raise concerns about your motivations. Employers prefer candidates who seem excited and confident about joining the team, rather than overly worried about potential problems.

**Examples to Avoid:**

- *"How long do employees typically stay with the company?"*

- *"Has there been a lot of turnover in this role?"*

**Better Approach:**
You can still ask about job stability in a more positive way by framing it around the company's growth and your long-term contributions.

- *"What opportunities exist for long-term growth within the company?"*

- *"How do you see this role evolving in the next few years?"*

## 6. Questions That May Come Across as Negative or Critical

While it's important to get a realistic sense of the work environment, asking questions that seem critical or overly negative can put the interviewer on the defensive and make the conversation uncomfortable.

**Examples to Avoid:**

- *"Why has this position been vacant for so long?"*
- *"I've read some negative reviews about your company online what's that all about?"*

**Better Approach:**
If you have concerns, frame your questions constructively. Focus on solutions and opportunities, rather than highlighting potential problems.

- *"Can you tell me more about the challenges faced by the team and how you are addressing them?"*
- *"What is your approach to employee feedback and continuous improvement within the company?"*

## 7. Overly Personal Questions

It's important to maintain professionalism during the interview. Asking overly personal questions about the interviewer's personal life or making them uncomfortable with intrusive inquiries can create an awkward dynamic and reduce your chances of being seen as a serious candidate.

**Examples to Avoid:**

- *"Do you have a family? How do you manage work-life balance here?"*
- *"What do you like to do outside of work?"*

**Better Approach:**
While you can build rapport by asking the interviewer about their experiences at the company, keep the questions professional and focused on the role or company culture.

- *"What has your career path within the company looked like?"*

- *"What do you enjoy most about working here?"*

## Conclusion

When preparing questions for an interview, focus on asking thoughtful, specific questions that reflect your interest in the role and company. Avoid questions that make you seem unprepared, overly self-focused, or negative. By steering clear of these potential pitfalls and asking insightful, strategic questions, you'll leave a positive impression and demonstrate your professionalism, enthusiasm, and suitability for the role.

## Chapter 6: Navigating Tricky Situations

### Dealing with Stress and Unexpected Questions

Interviews can be stressful, especially when you encounter difficult or unexpected questions. How you handle these moments often makes a lasting impression on the interviewer. In this section, we'll explore practical techniques to help you stay calm under pressure and manage challenging questions with confidence and poise.

### 1. Understanding the Nature of Unexpected Questions

Unexpected questions are designed to assess your critical thinking, problem-solving, and ability to remain composed under pressure. These questions might not always have a "right" answer, but interviewers are keen to see how you approach the challenge, how you articulate your thought process, and whether you maintain composure.

### Examples of unexpected questions:

- *"If you were a superhero, what power would you choose and why?"*
- *"How many golf balls could fit inside a Boeing 747?"*

- *"Tell me about a time when you disagreed with a manager. How did you handle it?"*

The purpose of such questions isn't to trip you up but to gain insight into your creativity, logic, and self-awareness. By understanding the intention behind these questions, you can frame your responses more effectively.

## 2. Staying Calm Under Pressure

The key to handling stress during an interview is learning to manage your mindset and body's response to pressure. When confronted with an unexpected question, a momentary pause to gather your thoughts is entirely acceptable and can be seen as a sign of maturity.

**Tips for remaining calm:**

- **Take a deep breath:** Pausing for a breath gives you time to collect your thoughts and centres your response, making it more structured and coherent.

- **Acknowledge the question:** If you need time to think, acknowledge the question by saying something like, *"That's an interesting question. Let me take a moment to consider."*

- **Maintain positive body language:** Even if you feel flustered, keep your body language confident. Sit up straight, make eye contact, and smile. Open, engaged body language signals confidence to the interviewer.

**Mindset techniques for managing stress:**

- **Reframe stress as excitement:** Rather than seeing stress as a negative force, try reframing it as excitement or a challenge. This mental shift can make you feel more empowered and motivated.

- **Visualise success before the interview:** Spend a few minutes before the interview visualising yourself answering tough questions with calmness and confidence. This mental rehearsal can boost your self-assurance.

### 3. Handling Unexpected Questions Gracefully

When an interviewer throws an unexpected or tricky question your way, how you respond is more important than the actual answer you give. It's okay to take a moment to think about your answer, and even if you don't know the answer, showing resilience and adaptability is key.

**Strategies for answering unexpected questions:**

- **Break down complex questions:** If faced with a challenging question, break it down into smaller parts to help structure your response. For example, if asked how you'd solve a complicated problem, you can outline your approach step by step.

**Example:**
*Question: "How many tennis balls can fit inside a school bus?"*
**Response:** *"I would start by estimating the volume of the bus, then calculate the approximate size of a tennis ball. Based on that, I could make an educated guess about how many could fit inside. While I don't have exact numbers, my approach would involve these calculations."*

- **Clarify or ask for more information:** If a question is unclear or open-ended, feel free to ask for clarification. This shows you're thoughtful and thorough in your approach.
  *"Could you clarify what aspect of the problem you'd like me to focus on?"*

- **Stay honest if you don't know the answer:** If you truly don't know the answer, be honest but frame your response in a way that highlights your willingness to learn.
  *"I'm not entirely sure of the answer to that, but I would research it by... (explain your approach)."*
- **Use the "bridge" technique:** If asked a tough question about a weakness or something uncomfortable, you can "bridge" to a positive by briefly addressing the issue and then steering the conversation toward your strengths.
  *"While I'm still improving my Excel skills, I'm confident in my ability to learn quickly, and I've successfully used it in previous roles for budgeting and data tracking."*

## 4. Turning Stressful Moments Into Opportunities

Stressful moments in interviews can be opportunities to show your emotional intelligence and ability to handle difficult situations calmly. How you react under pressure can signal to employers that you'll be able to perform well in high-stakes situations on the job.

**Turn stress into an opportunity by:**

- **Showing resilience:** If you don't know the answer to a difficult question, use it as an opportunity to demonstrate your problem-solving abilities, adaptability, and growth mindset.
  *"I don't have direct experience with that tool, but I've taught myself similar programs and am confident I can get up to speed quickly."*
- **Sharing examples of overcoming adversity:** When appropriate, relate the stressful moment back to a time when you successfully handled a challenging situation at work.

This showcases your resilience in real life situations.
*"There was a time in my previous job where I had to lead a project with very little notice. Although it was stressful, I relied on my organisational skills and team collaboration to ensure we met the deadline."*

### 5. Conclusion: Turning Nerves Into Strength

Interviews are designed to challenge candidates, but by preparing for unexpected questions and managing stress effectively, you can turn these tricky moments into opportunities to shine. Staying calm under pressure, framing your responses thoughtfully, and showcasing your adaptability can set you apart from other candidates. When you approach difficult questions with confidence and composure, you not only impress interviewers with your answers but also demonstrate your resilience and problem-solving skills key traits employers seek in top candidates.

Mastering these techniques can help you navigate even the toughest interviews and make a lasting, positive impression.

### Handling Panel Interviews and Video Interviews

Panel and video interviews present unique challenges, requiring specific preparation strategies to ensure success. In this section, we will explore how to navigate these interview formats, manage multiple interviewers, and present yourself confidently on camera. Mastering these formats will help you stand out as a well-rounded candidate who can adapt to different situations.

### 1. Handling Panel Interviews

A panel interview involves multiple interviewers, often from different departments or teams, asking questions in a coordinated fashion.

While it may feel more intense than a one-on-one interview, panel interviews offer a great opportunity to make an impression on a broader group within the organisation.

**Challenges of panel interviews:**

- **Multiple interviewers, different perspectives:** Each panellist may have their own interests and concerns based on their role within the company. One person may focus on technical skills, another on culture fit, and another on your problem-solving abilities.

- **Managing multiple questions:** You may receive back-to-back questions from different people, making it more challenging to keep track of the conversation and respond appropriately.

- **Maintaining engagement with everyone:** You need to balance your attention and engagement across the entire panel, not just with the person who asked the question.

**Strategies for success:**

- **Research the panel beforehand:** If possible, find out who will be on the panel and what their roles are within the organisation. Understanding their perspectives can help you anticipate the types of questions they may ask and tailor your responses accordingly.

**Example:** If one interviewer is from HR, expect questions about culture fit and soft skills. If another is a technical lead, prepare for more technical or role-specific questions.

- **Make eye contact with everyone:** When responding to a question, address the person who asked it first, but be sure to make eye contact with other members of the panel. This ensures you engage the entire group and demonstrate that you're comfortable interacting with multiple people.

- **Pace yourself when answering:** Since you may face rapid-fire questioning, take a moment to gather your thoughts before responding. It's okay to ask for clarification or confirmation if you feel unclear about a question. Maintain a steady, thoughtful pace to avoid feeling rushed.

*"That's a great question. To clarify, are you asking about my experience managing large projects, or would you prefer I focus on a specific example?"*

- **Acknowledge different perspectives:** Sometimes, different members of the panel may have conflicting viewpoints. For example, a hiring manager may ask about how you'd handle deadlines, while an HR representative asks about work-life balance. Acknowledge and balance both perspectives in your answers to show that you can meet expectations from different angles.

*"I believe deadlines are critical, and I've always prioritised meeting them. At the same time, I've found that maintaining a good balance ensures my team stays motivated and productive."*

- **Send tailored follow-ups:** After the interview, send a thank-you email to each panellist. Personalise each note by referencing something specific from your interaction with that person. This demonstrates attention to detail and appreciation for the time they invested.

### 2. Handling Video Interviews

Video interviews have become increasingly common in today's job market, offering convenience but also introducing specific challenges such as technical issues and the need to convey presence through a screen. Successfully navigating a video interview requires preparation and a strategic approach to presenting yourself online.

**Challenges of video interviews:**

- **Technical glitches:** Poor internet connection, audio problems, or other technical difficulties can disrupt the interview and distract from your performance.

- **Lack of physical presence:** Without being in the same room, it can be harder to build rapport and make a strong connection with the interviewer.

- **Maintaining engagement on camera:** It's easy to come across as distracted or disengaged during a video call, especially if you're not familiar with the format.

**Strategies for success:**

- **Test your technology in advance:** Ensure your camera, microphone, and internet connection are working properly. Test your setup by making video calls with friends or family to troubleshoot any issues. It's also helpful to have a backup plan, such as a phone number to call if technical problems arise.

**Checklist before the interview:**

- Stable internet connection
- Camera positioned at eye level
- Good lighting (preferably natural light)
- Clear, professional background

**Dress professionally, head to toe:** Even though the interviewer may only see you from the waist up, dressing professionally from head to toe helps you mentally prepare for the interview and prevents any mishaps if you need to stand up unexpectedly.

- **Create a distraction-free environment:** Ensure your space is quiet and free from interruptions. Let others in your household know you'll be in an interview, and silence your phone and notifications on your computer.

- **Maintain eye contact with the camera:** During a video interview, it's tempting to look at the screen instead of the camera. However, to simulate eye contact, focus on looking directly into the camera when speaking. This makes it feel more like a face-to-face conversation.

**Tip:** Place a sticky note near your camera to remind yourself to look at it during the conversation.

- **Use body language to enhance engagement:** Although you're sitting in front of a camera, your body language still matters. Sit up straight, smile, and use natural hand gestures to emphasise points. Avoid crossing your arms or slouching, as this can make you seem disengaged.

- **Speak clearly and at a moderate pace:** Audio quality can sometimes be a challenge in video interviews. To ensure your interviewer hears you clearly, speak at a moderate pace and enunciate your words. Don't be afraid to pause briefly between sentences to give the interviewer time to process your answers.

- **Build rapport despite the distance:** Building rapport over video can be more challenging than in person, but it's still possible. Begin by engaging in a little small talk to establish a connection. Compliment the interviewer's background or ask how their day is going to break the ice.

- **Prepare for lag or interruptions:** Internet delays can occasionally cause awkward pauses or interruptions. If this happens, remain calm and professional.

Acknowledge the issue, and if necessary, politely ask the interviewer to repeat their question or clarify what was missed.

*"I'm sorry, it looks like the connection was a bit delayed. Could you repeat the last part of your question?"*

**Conclusion**

Panel and video interviews require distinct skills to navigate effectively, but with the right preparation, you can thrive in these formats. In a panel interview, your ability to engage with multiple people, balance different perspectives, and stay composed is crucial. In a video interview, it's all about adapting to the online environment, managing technology, and using body language and communication skills to maintain presence.

By mastering these formats, you demonstrate your adaptability and professionalism qualities that will help you stand out to potential employers in an increasingly competitive job market.

**Strategies for Overcoming a Poor Start**

It's not uncommon to feel that an interview has started poorly perhaps you stumble over an initial question, struggle with nerves, or feel off-balance due to a challenging start. However, interviews are marathons, not sprints, and recovering from a rocky beginning is entirely possible. With the right mindset and strategies, you can turn things around and leave a positive lasting impression. Here's how to handle a poor start and regain control of the conversation.

**1. Recognise that a Poor Start Is Recoverable**

Many candidates make the mistake of thinking that one misstep early on means the entire interview is ruined. In reality, most interviewers expect candidates to have nerves at the beginning, and they are generally understanding.

What matters more is how you handle the rest of the interview. Recognising that a poor start can be recovered is the first step in overcoming it.

**Key mindset tips:**

- **Don't dwell on it:** One small mistake doesn't define the entire interview. Don't let a single slip up colour your confidence for the rest of the conversation. Shift your focus to the questions ahead.

- **Accept that it's normal:** Many candidates experience nerves early in an interview. Even seasoned professionals can falter at the start. Interviewers know this and often don't hold early mistakes against you if you regain your footing.

- **Stay positive:** Maintaining a positive, solution-oriented mindset is key. Instead of criticising yourself internally, remind yourself of your strengths and refocus on your overall performance.

### 2. Acknowledge the Mistake (If Necessary) and Move On

In some cases, if you've made a factual error or misunderstood a question, it's okay to briefly acknowledge it and correct yourself. This demonstrates honesty, self-awareness, and professionalism. However, you don't need to draw unnecessary attention to small, unimportant mistakes.

**Examples of addressing a mistake:**

- **Misunderstanding a question:**
  *"I realise I misunderstood your question earlier. To clarify, I actually have experience managing cross-functional teams in my last role, and I'd be happy to expand on that if needed."*

- **Factual error:**
  *"I misspoke earlier regarding the size of the budget I managed. The correct figure was £100,000 annually."*

- **If the mistake is minor:** In most cases, a minor mistake doesn't need to be acknowledged, especially if it doesn't affect the overall flow of the interview. Simply focus on improving your performance in the remaining questions.

## 3. Use Breathing Techniques to Regain Composure

A poor start can make you feel flustered, which may affect your ability to think clearly. One of the quickest ways to recover is to take a deep breath and use relaxation techniques to regain composure. This helps reduce anxiety and allows you to re-centre your focus.

**Simple breathing techniques:**

- **The 4-7-8 method:** Inhale quietly through your nose for 4 seconds, hold the breath for 7 seconds, and exhale completely through your mouth for 8 seconds. This can be done subtly during a brief pause in the interview or while the interviewer is speaking.

- **Pausing before answering:** If you feel rushed or off-balance, take a moment before answering the next question. A brief pause to collect your thoughts signals confidence, and you can use this time to focus on your breathing.

**Example:**
*"That's a great question. Let me take a moment to think about the best example."*

### 4. Focus on Highlighting Your Strengths

Once you've had a rough start, it's important to shift your focus to highlighting your strengths for the remainder of the interview. Look for opportunities to bring the conversation back to your key skills, experiences, and achievements. This can help the interviewer refocus on your value as a candidate rather than any early missteps.

**Strategies to emphasise strengths:**

- **Weave your strengths into your responses:** Whenever you're asked a question, find a way to incorporate your top skills or most relevant experiences into the answer.

**Example:**
*"In addition to my project management experience, one of my strengths is my ability to communicate complex ideas clearly, which helped in leading cross-departmental initiatives at my last company."*

- **Use the STAR method to demonstrate competencies:** For behavioural questions, use the STAR (Situation, Task, Action, Result) framework to structure your answers and demonstrate your strengths in action.

**Example:**
*"In my previous role, we faced a tight deadline on a major project (Situation). I was responsible for leading the team and delegating tasks (Task). I used my strong organisational skills to prioritise tasks and streamline communication (Action), and as a result, we delivered the project on time and under budget (Result)."*

## 5. Re-establish Rapport with the Interviewer

Building rapport with the interviewer can help smooth over a rocky start. If you feel that the interview began awkwardly or didn't start off on the right foot, make an effort to engage with the interviewer and create a positive, friendly dynamic as the conversation progresses.

**Tips for re-establishing rapport:**

- **Use active listening:** Show that you're fully engaged by listening closely to the interviewer's questions, nodding, and responding thoughtfully. Active listening builds rapport and shows that you value their input.

- **Inject some personality:** If appropriate, let a bit of your personality shine through. A small, light-hearted comment or a genuine smile can help ease tension and create a more relaxed environment.

**Example:**
*"That's an interesting question! It reminds me of a challenge I faced in a previous role. I actually enjoy tackling complex problems like this one."*

- **Ask insightful questions:** Toward the end of the interview, when it's your turn to ask questions, show genuine curiosity about the role, the company, and the team dynamics. Thoughtful questions can leave a lasting positive impression.

**Example:**
*"Can you tell me more about how your team collaborates across departments, and how this role would fit into that structure?"*

## 6. End on a Strong Note

Even if the start of the interview didn't go as planned, you have the opportunity to leave a lasting positive impression with a strong closing. Your parting words and the final impression you leave can often outweigh any earlier missteps.

**Strategies for ending strong:**

- **Summarise your value:** When asked if you have anything else to add at the end of the interview, take the opportunity to briefly summarise why you're the best fit for the role. Focus on your unique strengths and what you bring to the table.

*"I'd like to reiterate that with my experience in [specific skill] and my passion for [role/industry], I'm confident I could bring real value to your team and help drive the success of your upcoming projects."*

- **Thank the interviewer:** Always express gratitude for the opportunity to interview. A sincere and positive closing leaves a lasting impression of professionalism.

*"Thank you for taking the time to meet with me today. I'm very excited about the opportunity and appreciate your time and insights."*

- **Follow up with a tailored thank-you note:** After the interview, send a follow up email thanking the interviewer for their time. If you feel the interview started poorly but improved, you can subtly reinforce your enthusiasm and interest in the role in your note.

*"I truly appreciated the opportunity to speak with you today about the position. I'm even more excited about the possibility of joining your team and contributing to [company name]'s success."*

**Conclusion: Bouncing Back with Resilience**

A poor start in an interview is by no means a dealbreaker. By staying calm, refocusing on your strengths, and re-establishing rapport with the interviewer, you can recover and deliver a strong overall performance. Ultimately, how you handle adversity and setbacks says a lot about your resilience and professionalism traits that many employers value. Remember, interviews are judged in their entirety, and ending strong can more than make up for a rocky beginning.

## Chapter 7: Following Up and Negotiating Offers

Once the interview is over, many candidates mistakenly think their work is done. However, the follow up process is just as crucial as the interview itself. Crafting a standout thank you note and strategically handling the negotiation process can make all the difference in securing a job offer. In this chapter, we will explore how to follow up with professionalism, gratitude, and clarity, ensuring you remain top of mind for the employer and position yourself well for offer negotiations.

### Crafting a Standout Thank-You Note

The thank-you note is more than just a polite gesture; it's an opportunity to reinforce your interest in the position, highlight key strengths discussed during the interview, and differentiate yourself from other candidates. A well-crafted thank-you note can leave a lasting impression and increase your chances of getting an offer.

**Why send a thank-you note?**

- **Shows professionalism:** Following up demonstrates your professionalism and appreciation for the time the interviewer spent with you.

It also reflects positively on your interpersonal skills, which are often just as important as your technical abilities.

- **Reinforces interest:** A thank you note gives you another chance to express your enthusiasm for the role and the company, reaffirming that you're genuinely interested in the position.

- **Allows you to address missed points:** Sometimes, during an interview, you might not fully answer a question or forget to mention a key detail. The thank-you note is your opportunity to fill in any gaps or expand on points you wish you had discussed further.

**Key Elements of a Standout Thank-You Note:**

1. **Timeliness:** Send the note within 24 to 48 hours of the interview. This ensures that you're still fresh in the interviewer's mind and that your note arrives before they make their final decision.

2. **Personalisation:** Avoid sending a generic thank you note. Tailor it to the specific interviewer, referencing details from your conversation to show that you were actively engaged. If you interviewed with multiple people, send individualised notes to each, reflecting on your interaction with them.

**Example:**
"I really enjoyed our discussion about the innovative projects your team is working on, particularly the AI driven system for customer feedback. I'm excited about the prospect of contributing to this initiative."

3. **Express gratitude:** Start by thanking the interviewer(s) for their time and consideration. Acknowledge the effort they put into meeting with you, and express genuine appreciation for the opportunity.

**Example:**
*"Thank you so much for taking the time to meet with me yesterday. It was a pleasure learning more about [Company Name] and the exciting initiatives your team is spearheading."*

4. **Reiterate your interest:** Reaffirm your enthusiasm for the position and the company. Let the interviewer know that your interest has only grown after the conversation. Be specific about why you're excited about the role.

**Example:**
*"After our conversation, I'm even more enthusiastic about the possibility of joining your team as [Job Title]. I'm confident that my experience in [specific skill] aligns with your needs, and I'm excited to contribute to [a specific project or company goal]."*

5. **Highlight key strengths:** Briefly mention any key strengths or relevant experiences that you feel are important. Tie these to what the interviewer is looking for to further align yourself with the role.

**Example:**
*"I believe my background in [specific skill] and experience managing [relevant project] would enable me to make an immediate impact on [Company Name]'s goals."*

6. **Close on a positive note:** Finish by thanking the interviewer again and expressing your excitement about the next steps in the hiring process.

**Example:**
*"Thank you again for your time and consideration. I look forward to hearing from you soon and am excited about the opportunity to contribute to your team at [Company Name]."*

**Sample Thank-You Note:**

*Subject: Thank You – [Your Name] Interview for [Job Title]*

Dear [Interviewer's Name],

Thank you so much for taking the time to meet with me [yesterday/earlier this week] to discuss the [Job Title] position at [Company Name]. I thoroughly enjoyed our conversation and learning more about the exciting work your team is doing, particularly [specific project or detail discussed during the interview].

I'm very enthusiastic about the opportunity to contribute my experience in [mention a relevant skill, experience, or achievement discussed during the interview] to [specific goals or projects]. After our discussion, I'm even more confident that my background aligns well with the needs of your team, and I'm excited about the chance to work together on [specific company initiative].

Thank you again for your time and consideration. I look forward to the next steps and the possibility of joining your innovative team at [Company Name].

Best regards,
[Your Name]

**Common Pitfalls to Avoid**

While a thank you note is crucial, there are some common mistakes candidates should avoid to ensure their follow up is professional and effective:

- **Being too generic:** Sending a generic thank-you note without any personalisation can come across as insincere. Always reference specific details from the interview.

- **Waiting too long to send it:** If you wait more than a couple of days to send your note, it may lose its impact. Timeliness is essential.

- **Lengthy emails:** Keep the note concise. You don't need to rehash the entire interview just touch on key points and keep the tone friendly but professional.

- **Over-selling yourself:** While it's important to reiterate your strengths, avoid coming across as overly aggressive or sales-oriented. A balanced tone of confidence and humility is most effective.

- **Neglecting proofreading:** A typo in a thank-you note can leave a bad impression. Proofread carefully before sending.

Crafting a standout thank you note is a simple yet powerful tool in your job search. It allows you to reinforce your interest, clarify any points, and leave a lasting, positive impression on the interviewer. Combined with strong interview performance and thoughtful follow up, you position yourself as a thoughtful, detail oriented candidate.

### Managing Multiple Job Offers or Delays in Response

In today's competitive job market, it's not uncommon for candidates to find themselves in a fortunate but challenging position: receiving multiple job offers or waiting anxiously for a response after a promising interview. Knowing how to navigate these situations with professionalism and tact is crucial for maintaining positive relationships with employers and making the best decision for your career. In this section, we will explore strategies for handling both scenarios, ensuring you make thoughtful and well-informed decisions.

### 1. Handling Multiple Job Offers

Receiving more than one job offer is a great position to be in, but it also requires careful consideration. You want to ensure you make the right choice for your long-term career goals, while also handling communications with employers in a respectful manner. Here's how to manage this scenario.

**Step 1: Take Your Time (Within Reason)**

It's important to avoid making hasty decisions when you receive multiple job offers. While it's exciting to have options, take the time to carefully evaluate each one based on factors like company culture, role responsibilities, compensation, career growth, and work-life balance.

**Tactful approach to buying time:**

- **Ask for a decision deadline:** Most employers provide a deadline for accepting an offer, but if they haven't, politely ask for one. This gives you time to consider all offers.

**Example:**
*"Thank you so much for extending this offer. I'm very excited about the opportunity and appreciate the time to carefully consider it. Could you let me know the latest date by which you'd need my decision?"*

- **Request a short extension if needed:** If you need more time beyond the original deadline, it's possible to request an extension, but make sure the timeframe is reasonable. Not all employers may grant an extension, but if you ask professionally and have a valid reason, they may accommodate your request.

- **Example:**
  *"I'm very enthusiastic about the offer and am currently in the final stages of discussions with another potential employer. Would it be possible to extend the decision deadline by a few days so I can give each opportunity careful consideration?"*

**Step 2: Evaluate the Offers Thoroughly**

When comparing multiple offers, it's easy to focus solely on salary, but it's crucial to consider a range of factors. Think about both your short-term and long-term goals, the company's mission, the potential for career growth, and how the role fits into your overall life priorities.

**Key factors to consider:**

- **Company culture and values:** Does the company's mission align with your personal values? Will you enjoy working in their environment? Ask yourself how you felt during the interview process did the company seem supportive and aligned with your working style?

- **Work-life balance:** Consider the demands of each role and whether they fit your lifestyle. Will you have a reasonable work-life balance? Are there flexible working arrangements?

- **Career growth opportunities:** Which role offers better long-term potential for advancement, professional development, or skill-building? Sometimes, an offer with a slightly lower salary but greater career growth potential is more advantageous in the long run.

- **Compensation package:** Beyond salary, review benefits such as health insurance, retirement plans, bonuses, equity, paid time off, and other perks.

**Create a comparison chart:** Listing the pros and cons of each offer can help you make an informed decision. A simple table comparing salary, benefits, career growth, company culture, and other key factors can provide clarity.

### Step 3: Communicate Your Decision Respectfully

Once you've made your decision, it's important to communicate your choice to both the company you've chosen and the one(s) you're turning down. Be professional, express gratitude, and don't burn bridges—you never know when you might encounter the other employer again.

**Accepting the offer:**

- **Express enthusiasm:** Show that you're excited about the opportunity and grateful for the offer.

**Example:**
"I'm thrilled to accept the offer for the [Job Title] position at [Company Name]. Thank you for this incredible opportunity I'm very much looking forward to joining the team and contributing to the company's success."

**Declining the other offer(s):**

- **Be polite and appreciative:** Always express gratitude for the offer, even if you're turning it down. A courteous, professional tone helps maintain relationships.

**Example:**
"Thank you very much for offering me the [Job Title] position at [Company Name]. After careful consideration, I've decided to accept another offer that is a better fit for my career goals at this time. I sincerely appreciate the time and effort you've invested in the process and wish you and the team continued success."

## 2. Dealing with Delays in Response

On the other hand, it's also common for candidates to experience delays in hearing back from an employer after an interview. While waiting can be stressful, there are tactful ways to handle this situation and maintain a positive relationship with the employer.

### Step 1: Be Patient, But Know When to Follow Up

Employers often take longer than expected to make hiring decisions due to various internal factors, such as multiple rounds of interviews or approval processes. While it's important to be patient, it's also okay to follow up politely after a reasonable amount of time has passed.

**When to follow up:**

- If the interviewer provided a timeline during the interview (e.g., "We'll get back to you by the end of next week"), wait until that period has passed before following up. If they didn't give a specific timeframe, waiting about a week after the interview is generally appropriate.

**Example follow-up email:**
*"I wanted to follow up regarding the [Job Title] position. It was a pleasure speaking with you during the interview, and I'm excited about the opportunity to contribute to [Company Name]. I was wondering if there were any updates on the hiring timeline, and I'd be grateful for any information you could provide. Thank you again for your time."*

**Stay professional and avoid being pushy:** It's important to maintain a professional tone in your follow-up communication. Avoid sounding impatient or frustrated, as this can harm your relationship with the employer.

### Step 2: Continue Your Job Search

While waiting for a response, it's essential to keep your job search active. Don't put all your eggs in one basket continue applying to other positions and attending interviews. This ensures you don't lose momentum if the response is delayed or doesn't lead to an offer.

- **Stay open to new opportunities:** Even if you feel strongly about a particular role, it's smart to pursue multiple options to keep your chances of landing a great job high.

- **Consider backup offers carefully:** If you're waiting on your top choice but receive another offer, it's okay to communicate that you're in the process of waiting for responses from other companies. However, manage this tactfully to avoid jeopardising the backup offer.

**Example response to another offer while waiting:**
*"Thank you very much for extending the offer for the [Job Title] position. I'm very excited about this opportunity. I am currently awaiting the results of another interview process, and I was wondering if it would be possible to have a few extra days to make a decision. I want to ensure that I'm making the best long-term decision for my career."*

### Step 3: Know When to Move On

If you haven't heard back after multiple follow ups and an extended period has passed, it may be time to move on from that opportunity. While it can be disappointing, continuing to focus on active job leads is more productive. Keep your communication respectful, even if you decide to withdraw from the process.

**Example email withdrawing candidacy:**
*"I wanted to follow up to check in on the status of the [Job Title] position. I've sincerely appreciated the opportunity to interview and learn more about your team. However, as I have not heard back, I am moving forward with other opportunities. Thank you again for considering me for this role, and I hope our paths cross again in the future."*

**Conclusion: Mastering Job Offer Management**

Whether you're juggling multiple offers or dealing with delays in responses, handling these situations with professionalism and patience will reflect positively on you as a candidate. By evaluating job offers thoroughly, communicating clearly with employers, and continuing your search actively while waiting, you can make informed decisions that support your long-term career success. Managing this delicate process with confidence and strategy will ensure you secure the right opportunity for your future.

**How to Negotiate Salary and Benefits Effectively**

Negotiating your salary and benefits is a critical step in the hiring process, yet many candidates feel apprehensive about this conversation. While it can be uncomfortable, approaching salary negotiations with confidence and preparation can not only result in a better compensation package but also demonstrate your professionalism and assertiveness qualities that employers value. In this section, we'll explore strategies for negotiating effectively, from preparation to closing the deal.

**1. The Importance of Negotiating**

Salary negotiation isn't just about earning more money it's about making sure you're fairly compensated for your skills, experience, and the value you bring to the organisation.

Additionally, how you approach negotiations can set the tone for your future working relationship with your employer.

- **Compensation impacts career satisfaction:** Studies show that individuals who negotiate for a fair salary tend to feel more valued at work, which can lead to greater job satisfaction and long-term success.

- **Establishes a strong foundation:** Negotiating ensures that you start your new role with the right expectations, feeling confident that you're receiving a competitive package that reflects your market value.

**2. Do Your Research**

Before entering any negotiation, it's essential to know the industry standards and the value of your skills in the market. Going in with data driven insights empowers you to negotiate from a position of knowledge.

- **Research salary ranges:** Use reliable resources such as Glassdoor, PayScale, LinkedIn Salary, or industry reports to gather salary data for the role you're applying for. Consider your location, industry, years of experience, and specific skills to get a realistic range.

- **Evaluate the entire compensation package:** Don't focus solely on the base salary consider other benefits such as bonuses, health insurance, pension plans, stock options, paid time off, professional development, and flexible working arrangements. A comprehensive understanding of the full package helps you negotiate beyond just salary.

**Example:** *"Based on my research and industry standards, the typical salary range for a [Job Title] with my level of experience in [Location] is between £X and £Y. Given my background in [specific skills], I believe I should be compensated toward the higher end of that range."*

### 3. Timing is Everything

Timing plays a crucial role in salary negotiations. Bringing up salary too early in the interview process can be off putting to employers, but waiting too long can leave you without leverage. The right time to discuss salary is usually after you've received a formal job offer, or when the employer initiates the discussion.

- **Wait for the offer:** Let the employer make the first move. Once you have an offer in hand, you're in a stronger position to negotiate. If the interviewer asks about your salary expectations earlier in the process, respond by expressing flexibility while subtly deflecting:

**Example:**
*"I'm excited about this opportunity, and I'm sure we can come to an agreement on a fair salary once we've discussed the specifics of the role and my responsibilities."*

- **Be prepared to discuss numbers:** If pressed to provide a salary expectation, give a well-researched range rather than a specific figure. This gives you room to negotiate while showing that you're informed.

**Example:**
*"Based on my research and experience, I'm looking for a salary in the range of £X to £Y. However, I'm flexible and open to discussing the full compensation package."*

### 4. Express Enthusiasm While Negotiating

Employers want to hire candidates who are excited about the role, not just focused on the compensation. While negotiating, express your enthusiasm for the position and the company. This reassures the employer that you're not only interested in money but also genuinely invested in the role.

- **Show you're eager to contribute:** Frame your request for a higher salary within the context of your enthusiasm for the company and the value you bring.

**Example:**
"I'm very excited about the opportunity to join [Company Name] and contribute to [specific projects or goals]. Based on my skills and the value I can add, I believe a salary in the range of £X would be appropriate."

### 5. Leverage Your Unique Value

The key to effective negotiation is demonstrating how your unique skills and experience justify a higher salary. Employers are more likely to meet your requests if they clearly see the value you'll bring to the organisation.

- **Emphasise your strengths:** During the negotiation, remind the employer of your specific achievements and how they align with the company's needs. If you have rare or in-demand skills, highlight those to reinforce your value.

- **Use the offer as a baseline:** If the initial offer is below your expectations, frame your counteroffer based on how your skills exceed the baseline for the role.

**Example:**
"I appreciate the offer of £X. However, given my experience in [specific area] and my proven ability to [achievement], I believe a salary closer to £Y would be more reflective of my expertise."

## 6. Negotiate the Full Package, Not Just Salary

Salary is only one component of a compensation package. You can negotiate other benefits to make the offer more attractive if salary increases are limited. Consider options like signing bonuses, additional holiday time, flexible work arrangements, or professional development opportunities.

- **Explore non salary perks:** If the employer cannot meet your salary request, ask about enhancing other benefits. For example, you might negotiate for a performance based bonus, remote work days, or a faster path to salary reviews.

**Example:**
*"I understand that the salary offer of £X is firm, but would it be possible to discuss a performance-based bonus structure or additional paid time off?"*

- **Long-term incentives:** Ask about opportunities for salary increases based on performance or professional development opportunities, such as training, certifications, or attending industry conferences.

## 7. Be Willing to Compromise

Negotiation is a two-way street. While it's important to advocate for yourself, be prepared for some give and take. Enter negotiations with a clear understanding of your priorities whether that's base salary, benefits, or long-term growth and be willing to compromise on less critical factors.

- **Prioritise your must-haves:** Identify the non-negotiables that are essential to you (e.g., minimum salary) and the areas where you're willing to be flexible (e.g., remote working options).

- **Accept a reasonable offer:** If the employer meets most of your key requests, it may be best to accept, even if it's not a perfect match.

### 8. Stay Professional and Gracious

Regardless of the outcome, remain professional and gracious throughout the negotiation process. Whether the employer meets your salary demands or not, expressing gratitude for the offer and the opportunity to negotiate is essential.

- **Keep a positive tone:** Even if the final offer doesn't fully meet your expectations, maintain a positive and professional attitude. Accept or decline the offer with grace, ensuring you leave a good impression.

**Example (Accepting):**
*"Thank you so much for your flexibility and for working with me on the offer. I'm very excited to accept the position and contribute to the team."*

**Example (Declining):**
*"I appreciate the offer and the time you've taken to discuss compensation with me. After careful consideration, I've decided to pursue other opportunities that are more aligned with my current career goals."*

### Conclusion: Mastering Salary Negotiations

Negotiating salary and benefits is a critical skill that can significantly impact your career satisfaction and financial well-being. By preparing thoroughly, expressing your value clearly, and remaining professional throughout the process, you can secure a compensation package that reflects your worth. Mastering negotiation helps ensure that you start your new role on strong footing, confident that you're being compensated fairly for the contributions you will make.

## Chapter 8: Interview Skills for Different Contexts

Every interview is unique, shaped not only by the company and role but also by the context in which the interview takes place. Interviewing for an internal promotion, an entry level position, or a senior leadership role requires different strategies and preparation. In this chapter, we'll explore how to tailor your approach to suit these varying contexts, ensuring that you present yourself in the most appropriate and effective manner for the position you're seeking.

### Tailoring Your Approach for Internal Promotions

Interviewing for an internal promotion has a distinct dynamic from external interviews. Since you're already part of the organisation, you have an insider's knowledge of the culture, processes, and team, which can work to your advantage. However, the challenge often lies in transitioning from being viewed in your current role to being seen as capable of handling greater responsibility.

**Key Strategies:**

1. **Leverage Your Track Record**

One of the advantages of applying for an internal promotion is that your performance is known. Use this opportunity to highlight your achievements, contributions, and growth within the company. Provide specific examples of projects you've led, challenges you've overcome, and how you've contributed to company objectives.

**Example:**
*"In my current role, I managed the [Project Name], which resulted in a 15% increase in efficiency. This experience has prepared me to take on the greater responsibility required for [New Role]."*

2. **Demonstrate Leadership and Initiative**

Internal promotions often require you to step into a leadership role or take on more strategic tasks. Even if you're not applying for a formal leadership position, it's essential to demonstrate that you can think strategically, solve problems proactively, and guide others. Highlight instances where you've taken the initiative beyond your current job description.

**Example:**
*"During the [Team Challenge], I identified a workflow issue that was impacting delivery times. I initiated a process change, which reduced delays by 10% and improved overall efficiency."*

3. **Address Familiarity Bias**

One of the challenges of internal interviews is overcoming the perception that you're already defined by your current role. To counteract this, focus on discussing new skills you've developed, additional responsibilities you've taken on, and how you've prepared yourself for the next step in your career.

**Example:**
*"While I've been with the company for [X years], I've continuously sought out opportunities to expand my skills, including completing [specific training] and taking on additional responsibilities within the team."*

**Tailoring Your Approach for Entry-Level Positions**

For those entering the workforce or making a significant career shift, the challenge is often overcoming a lack of experience. However, employers hiring for entry-level roles understand that you may not have extensive professional experience and are instead looking for potential, enthusiasm, and a willingness to learn.

**Key Strategies:**

1. **Highlight Transferable Skills**

If you're applying for an entry level role, you may not have direct experience in the field, but you likely have transferable skills from education, internships, volunteer work, or part-time jobs. These skills can include communication, teamwork, problem solving, and time management. Be specific about how these abilities apply to the job you're pursuing.

**Example:**
*"While working part-time as a customer service assistant, I developed strong communication and problem-solving skills, which I know will be valuable in this role as I work closely with clients and colleagues."*

2. **Emphasise Your Willingness to Learn**

One of the key attributes employers look for in entry-level candidates is a willingness to learn and grow. Demonstrate your enthusiasm for the industry and your eagerness to develop professionally. Mention any relevant courses, certifications, or self-directed learning you've undertaken to prepare for the role.

**Example:**
*"Although I'm new to this field, I've completed several online courses in [Industry Area] and have been actively learning through [specific platforms or resources] to ensure I can hit the ground running."*

3. **Show Enthusiasm and Cultural Fit**

At the entry level, attitude often matters as much as aptitude. Employers want to see that you're genuinely excited about the company and role, and that you will fit into the organisational culture. Research the company's values and mission and be ready to articulate why you want to work there specifically.

**Example:**
*"I'm particularly drawn to [Company Name] because of your focus on innovation and commitment to sustainability, which align closely with my values and the direction I want my career to take."*

**Tailoring Your Approach for Senior Roles**

Interviews for senior positions come with a different set of expectations. At this level, it's not just about having the necessary skills and experience; it's about demonstrating leadership, vision, and the ability to drive strategic objectives. Senior candidates are expected to have a deep understanding of industry trends, and their interview performance must convey their readiness to lead and inspire others.

**Key Strategies:**

1. **Demonstrate Strategic Thinking**

Senior roles require you to think beyond the day-to-day operations and focus on the larger picture. During the interview, you'll need to showcase your ability to develop and implement long-term strategies that align with the company's goals. Provide examples of how you've previously led strategic initiatives and the impact they had on the organisation.

**Example:**
*"At [Previous Company], I led the development of a five-year growth plan that resulted in a 20% increase in market share. By focusing on emerging trends and customer insights, I was able to drive key changes that positioned the company for long-term success."*

2. **Highlight Leadership and People Management Skills**

For senior roles, leadership ability is paramount. Interviewers will be interested in your management style, how you handle team dynamics, and how you develop others. Discuss your experience in leading teams, managing conflict, and mentoring others to reach their full potential.

**Example:**
"In my role as [Previous Position], I managed a team of 15, helping to develop their skills and improve productivity by 12%. I believe in fostering a collaborative environment where every team member feels valued and motivated."

3. **Address Organisational Impact and Change Management**

Senior executives are often hired to lead change whether it's growing the business, improving operational efficiency, or responding to market shifts. Be prepared to discuss your experience in driving change within an organisation, including how you handle resistance and ensure smooth transitions.

**Example:**
"When tasked with implementing a new company-wide CRM system, I ensured clear communication at all levels, providing training and ongoing support. As a result, we saw a 25% improvement in customer satisfaction and a smoother sales process."

4. **Speak to Your Vision for the Future**

At senior levels, interviewers want to know not only how you'll perform in the current role but also how you envision the future of the department or company. Be prepared to share your insights into industry trends and how you would help steer the company towards long-term growth and success.

**Example:**

*"Given the rapid advancements in AI and automation, I believe [Company Name] is in a prime position to capitalise on these technologies. My goal is to drive innovation within the company, leveraging these trends to improve both operational efficiency and customer satisfaction."*

**Conclusion: Adapting Your Interview Skills to the Role**

Whether you're aiming for an internal promotion, starting your career, or stepping into a senior leadership role, adapting your interview approach to the context of the position is essential. The key is to recognise the specific expectations of the role and tailor your responses to highlight the most relevant skills and experiences. By doing so, you'll not only demonstrate your suitability for the position but also convey that you understand the unique demands of the role and are prepared to meet them head-on.

**Industry-Specific Interview Tips**

While core interview skills are universally applicable, each industry has its own set of expectations, challenges, and nuances that can affect the way you approach the interview. Tailoring your preparation to the specific industry you're entering will demonstrate your understanding of the field and help you stand out as a candidate. Below, we'll explore how to fine-tune your interview approach for various sectors, including healthcare, tech, and the arts.

**1. Healthcare Industry**

The healthcare sector is one of the most critical and fast-paced industries, where professionalism, empathy, and ethical behaviour are paramount. Whether you're applying for a clinical role, administrative position, or management role in healthcare, these tips will help you make the right impression.

**Key Tips:**

- **Focus on patient care and safety:** Whether you're a nurse, doctor, or healthcare administrator, patient care is central to healthcare roles. Be prepared to discuss how your work impacts patient outcomes, as well as your commitment to patient safety, empathy, and ethical decision-making.

**Example Question:**
*"How do you handle stressful situations when a patient's condition is deteriorating?"*
**Suggested Approach:**
Demonstrate calmness under pressure, explaining how you follow protocols, communicate effectively with the team, and ensure patient safety.

- **Highlight multidisciplinary collaboration:** Healthcare is a team based industry where you'll work alongside a variety of professionals. Show your ability to collaborate across departments whether with physicians, nurses, or administrative staff to ensure optimal patient outcomes.

- **Stay updated on healthcare policies and technology:** Healthcare is constantly evolving, and employers will expect you to stay current on the latest developments, whether it's new technology (like electronic health records) or changes in health policy. Demonstrating your awareness of industry shifts can set you apart.

**Example Question:**
*"What recent healthcare advancements do you think will have the biggest impact on patient care?"*
**Suggested Approach:**
Discuss specific technologies, such as telemedicine or AI, and explain how they can be applied to enhance patient experience or improve operational efficiency.

## 2. Tech Industry

The tech industry is known for its innovation, problem solving mindset, and a fast paced, ever evolving work environment. Interviews in this field tend to focus on both your technical expertise and your ability to think critically and creatively.

**Key Tips:**

- **Be ready for technical assessments:** Many tech interviews involve coding challenges, whiteboard exercises, or technical assessments. Practising for these is essential. If you're applying for a software development role, for example, you'll need to demonstrate fluency in programming languages relevant to the job, such as Python, Java, or C++.

**Example Question:**
"Solve this coding problem: Write a function that checks if a string is a palindrome."
**Suggested Approach:**
Break down the problem logically, explaining your thought process before diving into the code.

- **Demonstrate problem-solving abilities:** Many tech companies use situational questions or real-world scenarios to gauge how well you can troubleshoot and think critically. It's crucial to articulate how you approach complex issues, test hypotheses, and arrive at solutions.

**Example Question:**
"Describe a time when you faced a major challenge with a system implementation. How did you resolve it?"
**Suggested Approach:**
Walk through the problem, the methods you used to diagnose the issue, and the solution you implemented, with a focus on the outcome and impact.

- **Highlight collaboration and soft skills:** Although tech roles are often highly technical, employers are increasingly looking for candidates with strong communication and teamwork skills. Be ready to explain how you work with non-technical teams, communicate technical concepts, and contribute to a collaborative work culture.

### 3. Arts and Creative Industries

The arts and creative sectors, which encompass industries like media, design, and performance arts, are highly subjective and often rely on portfolio work to demonstrate skills. Creativity, collaboration, and the ability to meet deadlines are key elements for success in these fields.

**Key Tips:**

- **Showcase your portfolio:** In creative industries, your portfolio is your strongest asset. Be prepared to walk through your work, explaining the thought process, design principles, or artistic influences behind each piece. Tailor your portfolio to the specific role and employer to demonstrate your understanding of their brand and needs.

**Example Question:**
*"Can you talk us through the creative process for your [specific project]?"*
**Suggested Approach:**
Explain your inspiration, the design process, any challenges you encountered, and how you addressed client feedback or adapted your work.

- **Highlight collaboration and client management:** Creative roles often involve working closely with clients, other creatives, or teams from different departments.

Employers will want to see how you manage client relationships, handle creative direction, and work collaboratively on projects.

**Example Question:**
*"How do you handle feedback that differs from your artistic vision?"*
**Suggested Approach:**
Demonstrate your flexibility and ability to take constructive criticism. Emphasise how you balance client feedback with your creative integrity to produce a final product that satisfies all stakeholders.

- **Stay informed on industry trends:** Creative industries are heavily influenced by trends in design, media, and technology. Be ready to discuss the latest movements, tools, or software (e.g., Adobe Creative Suite, Pro Tools) relevant to your field.

### 4. Finance and Banking

In the finance sector, interviews often focus on technical knowledge, analytical skills, and ethics. Candidates need to demonstrate not only their quantitative abilities but also their attention to detail and understanding of regulatory standards.

**Key Tips:**

- **Master financial knowledge and analysis:** Be prepared for detailed questions on financial modelling, investment strategies, or accounting principles, depending on the role. Employers in finance expect you to have a firm grasp of numbers and the ability to make data-driven decisions.

**Example Question:**
*"How would you value a company for a potential acquisition?"*

**Suggested Approach:**
Discuss the valuation methods (e.g., DCF, comparable companies, precedent transactions) and the rationale for selecting one over the other based on the context of the acquisition.

- **Demonstrate your understanding of risk and compliance:** The finance industry is heavily regulated, and employers need to ensure that candidates understand compliance requirements, ethical standards, and risk management processes. Be prepared to discuss how you navigate regulatory environments or mitigate risks in your work.

**Example Question:**
*"Describe a time when you identified a potential risk in a transaction or process and how you addressed it."*

**Suggested Approach:**
Highlight your attention to detail and proactive approach to ensuring compliance and mitigating financial or legal risks.

- **Showcase problem-solving and decision making skills:** Finance roles often require quick, informed decision-making based on complex data sets. Employers will want to know how you approach these challenges and ensure accuracy in high-pressure situations.

## 5. Education

The education sector, whether in teaching, administration, or academic support, places a strong emphasis on communication, empathy, and the ability to engage with diverse audiences. Flexibility and a passion for learning are key attributes.

**Key Tips:**

- **Emphasise teaching philosophy and pedagogy:** If you're applying for a teaching or training role, be prepared to discuss your approach to teaching, classroom management, and student engagement. Schools and educational institutions want to understand how you create an inclusive, supportive learning environment.

**Example Question:**
*"How do you differentiate instruction for students with varying levels of ability?"*
**Suggested Approach:**
Discuss specific strategies you use to ensure all students can succeed, such as differentiated learning plans or using technology to personalise education.

- **Demonstrate adaptability and problem-solving:** Education is often unpredictable, requiring quick thinking and adaptability to meet the needs of students and manage challenges. Be prepared to give examples of how you handle unexpected situations or solve problems on the spot.

**Example Question:**
*"Tell us about a time when you had to adapt your lesson plan due to unforeseen circumstances."*
**Suggested Approach:**
Explain the steps you took to adjust the lesson, keep students engaged, and ensure that learning outcomes were still achieved.

- **Highlight collaboration with parents and staff:** In education, building relationships with parents, staff, and other educators is crucial. Be ready to discuss how you foster these connections to create a supportive learning environment for students.

## Conclusion: Tailoring Your Interview to the Industry

Every industry has unique expectations and requirements for candidates, and understanding these nuances can give you a competitive edge. Whether you're preparing for a tech interview that requires coding assessments, a healthcare interview focused on patient care, or an arts role where your portfolio takes centre stage, tailoring your interview skills to align with the specific demands of the sector is essential. By demonstrating both your expertise and your understanding of industry specific challenges, you'll show employers that you're the right fit for the job.

## Handling Interviews for Freelance or Contract Work

Interviews for freelance or contract roles are often different from traditional job interviews. In these scenarios, employers are not only evaluating your skills but also assessing your ability to work independently, manage time efficiently, and deliver high-quality results without constant oversight. The hiring process can be more project-oriented, and negotiations around terms, timelines, and compensation play a bigger role. Here's how to approach interviews for freelance or contract work.

### 1. Highlight Your Expertise and Specialised Skills

Unlike traditional employment, where an employer might hire someone with broader skill sets, freelance and contract positions often require specific expertise. You need to position yourself as a specialist in the field or service you are offering, rather than a generalist. Clients want someone who can quickly deliver results without extensive training or onboarding.

**Key Tips:**

- **Be concise and clear about your specialisation:** Clearly explain what makes you an expert in the specific field. Provide examples of similar projects you've worked on and highlight your unique strengths.

**Example Question:**
*"What kind of projects have you worked on in the past?"*
**Suggested Approach:**
Discuss a few key projects that align with the prospective client's needs. Focus on the impact you had and the tangible results you delivered, whether it was increasing sales, improving processes, or meeting tight deadlines.

- **Showcase your portfolio:** Freelance interviews often rely heavily on showcasing your previous work. Your portfolio is your strongest evidence of competency and expertise. Make sure it's well-organised and tailored to the type of work the client needs.

**Example Question:**
*"Can you show me examples of similar work you've done?"*
**Suggested Approach:**
Walk through 2-3 examples that are relevant to the job, providing details about the project scope, challenges, and how you met or exceeded client expectations.

## 2. Demonstrate Your Independence and Problem-Solving Skills

Since freelancers and contractors typically work without much supervision, clients want to ensure that you can handle the entire process independently from concept to execution while solving problems along the way. The ability to manage your own time, overcome obstacles, and meet deadlines is critical.

**Key Tips:**

- **Provide examples of self-directed projects:** Clients value freelancers who can take ownership of projects and deliver without needing constant input. Share examples where you took initiative, managed your own time, and successfully completed a project from start to finish.

**Example Question:**
*"How do you stay motivated and organised when working independently?"*
**Suggested Approach:**
Explain your approach to time management, your work process, and how you keep yourself motivated to meet deadlines. You might mention tools you use (e.g., project management software like Trello, Asana) to stay on track.

- **Emphasise your problem-solving ability:** Clients are often looking for freelancers who can solve challenges on their own without adding extra burden to the client. Be ready to explain how you troubleshoot issues or adapt when things don't go according to plan.

**Example Question:**
*"What do you do if a project takes longer than expected or hits a snag?"*
**Suggested Approach:**
Highlight your proactive approach to problem solving and your ability to communicate potential delays early. Share examples of how you've solved past challenges, ensuring the client still received the results they needed.

### 3. Be Prepared to Discuss Project Scope and Pricing

Unlike full-time positions, freelance work often involves negotiating the scope of the project, deadlines, and payment terms. Freelancers are expected to have a clear understanding of what they are offering and to be able to communicate it to potential clients in a professional way.

**Key Tips:**

- **Define the project scope clearly:** Be prepared to discuss deliverables, timelines, and what is included in your services. Make sure you and the client are on the same page to avoid scope creep (when additional tasks are added without proper adjustments to the contract).

**Example Question:**
*"How long will this project take, and what can we expect as deliverables?"*
**Suggested Approach:**
Provide a clear timeline, breaking the project into phases or milestones, and explain what the client will receive at each stage. Discuss any potential factors that could affect the deadline and how you'll handle them.

- **Be transparent about your rates:** Clients want to know upfront what your services will cost and what's included in your rate. Be confident in your pricing but also be open to negotiating if necessary. If the project requires a flexible rate (e.g., for additional hours or scope), explain your terms clearly.

**Example Question:**
*"What are your rates and payment terms?"*

**Suggested Approach:**
State your rate confidently, explaining how it reflects your expertise and the value you provide. Be open to discussing terms like down payments or milestone-based payments to ensure you're compensated fairly throughout the project.

### 4. Highlight Communication and Client Management Skills

Clients need to feel confident that you can communicate effectively and that they won't be left in the dark about the project's progress. Freelancers often work remotely, making communication even more important. It's critical to show that you're accessible, responsive, and able to manage client expectations.

**Key Tips:**

- **Set expectations for communication:** During the interview, explain how and how often you'll update the client on project progress. Discuss your preferred communication methods, such as email, video calls, or project management tools.

**Example Question:**
*"How will we stay updated on the project's progress?"*
**Suggested Approach:**
Mention how you regularly update clients through reports, meetings, or project management tools. Give examples of how you've successfully managed client communication on past projects.

- **Manage client expectations from the start:** Freelancers need to be skilled at managing client expectations regarding deadlines, revisions, and feedback.

Be proactive in discussing how you'll handle feedback and ensure that both parties have a mutual understanding of what's expected.

**Example Question:**
*"How do you handle revisions or feedback during a project?"*
**Suggested Approach:**
Explain your process for incorporating client feedback while ensuring that the project remains on track. You might mention offering a set number of revisions to avoid endless adjustments and scope changes.

**5. Focus on Building Trust and Professionalism**

Freelancers often have a brief window to build trust during interviews. Clients are not just looking at your skills but also assessing whether you are reliable, professional, and someone they can depend on for future projects.

**Key Tips:**

- **Demonstrate reliability and past client satisfaction:** Share testimonials or case studies that demonstrate your ability to deliver quality work on time and on budget. If you've worked with well-known clients or had repeat business, highlight that to build credibility.

**Example Question:**
*"Can you share feedback from past clients?"*
**Suggested Approach:**
Mention positive testimonials or specific instances where clients praised your work. Provide concrete examples of how your work positively impacted their business, whether through increased sales, brand visibility, or efficiency improvements.

- **Present yourself as a long-term partner:** Even if you're being hired for a short-term project, clients value freelancers who think about the big picture. Show that you're invested in the client's success by discussing how you could support their future needs or help them beyond the current project.

**Example Question:**
*"How do you see your role contributing to our long-term goals?"*
**Suggested Approach:**
Explain how your work aligns with the company's broader objectives and how you can add value in the long term. This could open doors to more projects or ongoing collaboration.

**Conclusion: Excelling in Freelance and Contract Interviews**

Interviewing for freelance or contract work requires a shift in focus from traditional job interviews. You need to emphasise your specific expertise, ability to work independently, and value proposition as a service provider. By preparing thoroughly for questions about your past work, project management skills, and client communication, you'll be able to position yourself as the ideal freelance professional for the job. Furthermore, being clear and upfront about rates, timelines, and deliverables will help build trust and set you apart as a professional.

**Conclusion: Becoming an Interview Master**

Mastering the art of interviews is not a destination but a journey. It's a continuous process of self-improvement, learning, and refining your approach. Whether you're seeking a new role, aiming for a promotion, or negotiating a freelance contract, developing strong interview skills is essential to your professional success. The more interviews you engage in, the more you learn, grow, and become adept at presenting yourself effectively.

## 1. Continuous Improvement: Learning from Feedback and Failed Interviews

Even the most experienced professionals encounter interviews that don't go as planned. Whether it's receiving constructive feedback or facing outright rejection, every interview successful or not provides valuable lessons.

The key to becoming an interview master lies in your ability to take those lessons and improve.

**Key Strategies for Continuous Growth:**

- **Solicit Feedback:** After each interview, particularly if you don't get the job or contract, don't hesitate to ask for feedback from the interviewer. Understanding their perspective on what went well and what didn't can help you pinpoint areas for improvement. While not every employer will provide detailed feedback, those that do can offer invaluable insights.

**Example Approach:**
*"Thank you for the opportunity to interview for the position. I would appreciate any feedback you can share to help me improve for future interviews."*

- **Self-Reflection and Honest Assessment:** Take the time to reflect on each interview. Consider the questions you were asked, how you responded, and how comfortable you felt during the process. Were there any areas where you felt less confident? Did you struggle with certain types of questions? Honest self-assessment allows you to focus on the areas that need attention.

**Questions to Ask Yourself:**

- Did I communicate my key strengths clearly?
- Were there any questions where I stumbled or hesitated?
- How well did I tailor my answers to the role or company?
- Was my non-verbal communication (e.g., body language) aligned with my words?

**Learn from Rejection:** Every rejection is an opportunity to improve. While being turned down for a role can be disappointing, it's important to view each rejection as part of the learning curve. Reevaluate your approach and make adjustments where necessary. Did the interviewer point out a gap in your qualifications or a misalignment with the role? Use that feedback to strengthen your pitch for future opportunities.

## 2. Embrace a Growth Mindset

Adopting a growth mindset believing that your skills and abilities can be developed with time and effort will help you stay motivated and resilient. Interview skills are like any other professional skill: they improve with practice, feedback, and persistence.

- **View challenges as opportunities:** If a particular interview technique or question stumps you, take it as an opportunity to learn rather than a sign of failure. Research ways to improve, practice with a mentor, or role-play interviews to build confidence.

- **Commit to lifelong learning:** Stay informed about evolving interview practices, changes in industry standards, and new techniques. The world of work is constantly evolving, and so too are the ways in which companies assess candidates.

By keeping up to date, you'll ensure that your interview skills remain relevant and sharp.

### 3. Practice, Practice, Practice

Becoming an interview master doesn't happen overnight. It requires continuous practice, rehearsal, and exposure to different interview scenarios. Even if you're not actively job hunting, consider taking mock interviews or practising with friends, colleagues, or career coaches.

The more comfortable you become in an interview setting, the more naturally you'll be able to present yourself during real opportunities.

- **Rehearse answers to common questions:** Preparing responses to common questions, like "Tell me about yourself" or "What are your weaknesses?", ensures that you're not caught off guard. As you practice, focus on delivering concise and clear answers that demonstrate your skills, achievements, and value.

- **Role-play tricky situations:** Simulate challenging interview scenarios, such as panel interviews, tough behavioural questions, or handling a poor start. By practising in a low-stakes environment, you'll be better equipped to navigate difficult situations with poise.

### 4. Building Resilience for Long-Term Success

The path to mastering interviews will include moments of doubt, frustration, and rejection, but building resilience is essential for long-term success. Understand that setbacks are part of the journey, not a reflection of your worth or capabilities. By cultivating resilience, you'll be able to maintain focus on your goals and bounce back from disappointment stronger than before.

**Key Resilience Tips:**

- **Maintain perspective:** Not every interview will result in a job offer, and that's okay. Keep in mind that sometimes rejection has nothing to do with your performance it may be due to internal hiring, budget cuts, or a better fit with another candidate. Stay focused on improving and preparing for the next opportunity.

- **Celebrate small wins:** Even if you don't get the job, celebrate the progress you're making. Did you feel more confident? Were your answers more polished than in previous interviews? Recognise the growth and give yourself credit for the improvements along the way.

**Conclusion: The Path to Interview Mastery**

Becoming an interview master is an ongoing journey, one built on self-reflection, constant improvement, and perseverance. While interviews can be nerve-wracking, they are also opportunities to learn more about yourself, improve your communication, and build resilience. The key is to approach each interview as a stepping stone towards your ultimate goal.

By committing to continuous learning, embracing feedback, practising regularly, and maintaining a growth mindset, you'll not only increase your chances of landing the job but also become a more confident, adaptable, and skilled professional. Remember, every interview, regardless of the outcome, is a valuable opportunity to refine your skills and get one step closer to mastering the art of the interview.

**Staying Prepared for Future Opportunities**

The job market is ever-changing, and career opportunities can arise when you least expect them.

Whether you are actively seeking a new role or simply keeping your options open, staying prepared for future opportunities ensures that you're ready to make the most of them when they appear. Here's how you can keep your interview skills sharp and stay proactive in positioning yourself for future success.

**1. Keep Your Resume and LinkedIn Profile Updated**

One of the easiest yet most effective ways to stay prepared is by regularly updating your resume and LinkedIn profile. Even if you're not actively job hunting, it's wise to reflect your latest accomplishments, skills, and experience in these documents. This will ensure that you're always ready to apply for new roles or be discovered by recruiters.

**Key Strategies:**

- **Regular updates:** Set aside time every few months to review and update your resume and LinkedIn profile. Add any new skills, certifications, projects, or achievements to reflect your growth.

- **Tailored content:** Customise your resume and profile to highlight the most relevant skills and experience for the type of opportunities you're interested in. Even if you're currently in a different role, ensure that your profile speaks to your desired future direction.

**Pro Tip:** Keeping your LinkedIn profile active and engaging (e.g., sharing industry news, writing articles, or commenting on posts) can boost your visibility to potential employers and recruiters.

**2. Build and Maintain Your Professional Network**

Networking plays a crucial role in uncovering job opportunities and staying connected to industry trends.

Building relationships within your industry can open doors to new roles, collaborations, and insider information on job openings before they're advertised.

**Key Strategies:**

- **Engage with industry peers:** Attend conferences, webinars, and networking events regularly to meet professionals in your field. Even informal conversations can lead to future job prospects.

- **Stay active online:** Engage with your network on platforms like LinkedIn by sharing insights, participating in discussions, and congratulating others on their achievements. This keeps you on their radar for potential opportunities.

- **Foster long-term relationships:** Don't just reach out to people when you need something build genuine, long-term connections by offering value and support. This way, when opportunities arise, your network is more likely to think of you.

### 3. Stay Informed About Industry Trends and Market Changes

Being aware of the latest trends and changes in your industry will help you stay competitive in the job market. Employers value candidates who are knowledgeable about current developments and who demonstrate an interest in the future of the industry.

**Key Strategies:**

- **Regular reading:** Subscribe to industry publications, blogs, or newsletters to stay updated on emerging trends, technological advancements, and changes in the job market.

- **Continuing education:** Take courses, attend workshops, or earn certifications to keep your skills relevant. Lifelong learning shows employers that you're committed to staying current and improving your expertise.

**Pro Tip:** Highlight your continuous learning on your resume and LinkedIn profile. This signals to employers that you are proactive and invested in your professional growth.

### 4. Practise Your Interview Skills Regularly

Even when you're not actively interviewing, it's important to keep practising your interview skills so that you don't feel rusty when the time comes. Regular practice ensures that you remain confident and articulate in expressing your strengths, experiences, and value.

**Key Strategies:**

- **Mock interviews:** Set up mock interviews with a mentor, career coach, or trusted colleague to stay sharp. Ask for feedback on your responses, body language, and overall presentation.

- **Self-reflection:** Revisit common interview questions and tailor your answers to highlight your most recent accomplishments and growth. This will help you craft polished, relevant responses for future opportunities.

**Pro Tip:** Consider recording yourself during mock interviews to identify areas for improvement, such as filler words, body language, or tone.

### 5. Strengthen Your Personal Brand

Your personal brand is how you present yourself to the professional world and how others perceive your skills, experience, and values.

By actively managing and refining your personal brand, you position yourself as an attractive candidate for future roles and opportunities.

**Key Strategies:**

- **Define your brand:** Be clear about your core strengths, values, and the unique value you bring to the table. Ensure that your personal brand aligns with your career goals.

- **Showcase your expertise:** Write articles, create content, or speak at industry events to establish yourself as a thought leader. By building a strong online presence, you increase the likelihood of being noticed by recruiters or potential employers.

**Pro Tip:** Social media platforms like LinkedIn, Twitter, and personal blogs are powerful tools for developing your personal brand. Use them to share your insights and demonstrate your passion for your industry.

### 6. Be Ready to Act Quickly When Opportunities Arise

Sometimes, the best opportunities come with little warning. To take full advantage, you need to be able to act quickly whether that means submitting your resume, scheduling an interview, or jumping into a conversation with a hiring manager.

**Key Strategies:**

- **Organise your job search materials:** Keep your resume, cover letter templates, and portfolio in easily accessible and editable formats, so you can quickly tailor them to specific job opportunities when they arise. Having these materials on hand will save you time and ensure you're always ready to apply promptly.

- **Prepare a go-to elevator pitch:** Have a concise introduction ready that summarises who you are, your skills, and your career goals. This will allow you to confidently introduce yourself when networking or speaking to potential employers, even on short notice.

- **Keep track of key contacts:** Maintain a list of industry contacts, recruiters, and mentors who might be able to inform you of job openings or recommend you for positions. Staying in touch with these individuals ensures that when opportunities come up, you're top of mind.

### 7. Maintain a Proactive, Long-Term Outlook

Staying prepared for future opportunities is about consistently positioning yourself as a strong candidate, even when you're not actively job hunting. By keeping your skills, network, and personal brand up to date, you can approach future interviews with confidence and ease.

**Key Strategies:**

- **Set career goals:** Periodically revisit your career goals to ensure that you're staying on track and aligning your preparation efforts with your aspirations. Adjust your plans as necessary to reflect changes in your industry or personal interests.

- **Track your progress:** Document your accomplishments, challenges, and feedback from interviews and professional experiences. This ongoing self-reflection will help you identify areas of improvement and stay motivated to reach the next level in your career.

**Pro Tip:** Keeping a professional journal or using a career tracker app can help you stay organised and provide valuable material when updating your resume or preparing for interviews.

By following these steps and maintaining a proactive approach, you'll always be ready to seize new opportunities as they come your way. Whether you're aiming for your dream job, exploring new industries, or considering a freelance gig, staying prepared ensures you're always positioned for success.

## Appendices: Sample Interview Questions and Answers

Having well-prepared answers to common interview questions can make a significant difference in how you present yourself to potential employers. While every interview is unique, being familiar with common questions and understanding how to tailor your responses to showcase your strengths will give you a strong foundation for success.

### 1. Tell Me About Yourself.

This is often the first question asked in interviews and sets the tone for the conversation. The key here is to give a concise, relevant summary of your career and skills.

**Sample Answer:**

*"I have over five years of experience in project management, with a strong focus on healthcare initiatives. In my current role as a project manager for XYZ Health Solutions, I lead cross-functional teams to implement software solutions aimed at improving patient care. One of my key achievements was overseeing the successful rollout of an electronic health records system that reduced administrative time by 20%. I'm particularly drawn to this role because of your company's emphasis on innovative healthcare solutions, and I'm excited about the opportunity to bring my experience and passion for healthcare improvement to your team."*

## 2. What Are Your Greatest Strengths?

When discussing strengths, focus on skills that are relevant to the role. Be sure to provide examples to illustrate your strengths in action.

**Sample Answer:**

*"One of my greatest strengths is my ability to manage complex projects under tight deadlines. For example, in my last position, I led a team in delivering a critical software update two weeks ahead of schedule, which resulted in a 15% increase in operational efficiency. I'm also highly adaptable, which has allowed me to navigate changing priorities effectively, ensuring that both short- and long-term goals are met without compromising quality."*

## 3. What Is Your Biggest Weakness?

This can be a tricky question. The best approach is to discuss a real weakness but also highlight the steps you're taking to improve it.

**Sample Answer:**

*"I sometimes struggle with delegating tasks because I like to ensure that everything is done to a high standard. However, I've recognised that this isn't always sustainable, especially when managing larger teams. I've been working on this by actively identifying tasks that can be delegated and trusting my team members to handle them. I've also begun incorporating regular feedback sessions to ensure that everything stays on track."*

## 4. Why Do You Want to Work Here?

To answer this effectively, show that you've done your research on the company and align your career goals with their mission.

**Sample Answer:**

*"I'm drawn to this company because of your dedication to sustainability and innovative business practices.*

*I admire the way you've incorporated environmental responsibility into your product line, and I believe that my background in sustainable product development aligns perfectly with your goals. I'm excited about the prospect of working in an organisation that not only values growth but also prioritises ethical practices."*

### 5. Where Do You See Yourself in Five Years?

Employers want to see that you have ambition and that your goals align with the company's objectives.

**Sample Answer:**

*"In five years, I see myself growing within this company, ideally in a leadership role where I can contribute to both strategic decision-making and team development. I'm particularly excited about the opportunity to continue advancing my skills in project management while also mentoring junior team members. My goal is to help drive the company's long-term success while continuing to develop as a professional."*

### 6. Tell Me About a Time You Handled a Challenging Situation.

This is a behavioural question where the STAR method (Situation, Task, Action, Result) can be especially useful.

**Sample Answer (Using the STAR Method):**

*"In my previous role, we encountered a significant challenge when our project's timeline was shortened by two weeks due to an unexpected client deadline (Situation). As the project lead, my task was to ensure we still met the deadline without compromising quality (Task).*

*I immediately organised a meeting with the team to re-prioritise tasks and identify areas where we could streamline our process. We also reached out to the client to clarify their key priorities (Action).*

*In the end, we delivered the project on time, and the client was highly satisfied with the results, which led to an extended contract for future work (Result)."*

### 7. Why Are You Leaving Your Current Job?

When answering this question, focus on the positive aspects of what you're looking for, rather than the negatives of your current or previous role.

**Sample Answer:**

*"I've really enjoyed my time at my current company and have learned a great deal. However, I'm looking for a new challenge that will allow me to continue growing professionally. I'm particularly excited about this opportunity because it offers the chance to work on larger, more complex projects, which aligns with my long-term career goals."*

### 8. How Do You Handle Stress or Pressure?

Employers want to know how well you cope with challenging situations and whether you can remain productive and focused.

**Sample Answer:**

*"I find that having a structured approach to managing stress helps me stay focused and productive. I prioritise tasks by urgency and importance, and I make sure to communicate regularly with my team to ensure everyone is aligned on our objectives. For example, during a particularly busy period at my last job, I had to manage multiple high-priority projects simultaneously.*

*By breaking the projects into smaller tasks and setting clear timelines, I was able to complete everything on time without feeling overwhelmed."*

## 9. What Are Your Salary Expectations?

When discussing salary, it's important to be tactful. Research the market rate for the position and be prepared to offer a range.

**Sample Answer:**

*"Based on my research and understanding of the role and responsibilities, I believe a salary range between £45,000 and £55,000 is in line with the market for someone with my experience and skills. However, I'm open to discussing this further based on the specifics of the role and the overall compensation package."*

## 10. Do You Have Any Questions for Us?

This is your opportunity to demonstrate interest in the company and role. Asking thoughtful questions can leave a lasting impression on the interviewer.

**Sample Questions to Ask:**

- "What does success look like for this position in the first six months?"
- "Can you tell me more about the team I'll be working with?"
- "How do you support employee growth and development?"
- "What are the company's current priorities and how does this role contribute to them?"

These sample questions and answers provide a foundation for your interview preparation. Adjust your responses to reflect your own experiences and the specifics of the role, and you'll be well-equipped to make a strong impression.

**Appendices: Interview Checklists**

Being well-prepared for an interview can significantly boost your confidence and performance. A clear and organised checklist ensures that you don't overlook any critical steps in your preparation process. Below are comprehensive checklists to help you prepare for various stages of the interview process.

**Pre-Interview Checklist:**

This checklist covers everything you need to do before your interview to ensure you're ready to make a strong impression.

1. **Research the Company:**
    - Visit the company's website to learn about their mission, values, and products/services.
    - Review recent news articles, press releases, or company blog posts.
    - Understand the company culture, structure, and key stakeholders.
    - Familiarise yourself with the industry, competitors, and current market trends.

2. **Understand the Role:**
    - Carefully read the job description and identify the required skills and responsibilities.
    - Highlight keywords from the job posting to use in your answers.

- Understand how the role fits within the organisation's overall structure.

3. **Prepare Your Answers:**
    - Practise responses to common interview questions (e.g., "Tell me about yourself," "What are your strengths/weaknesses?").
    - Prepare examples using the STAR method (Situation, Task, Action, Result) for behavioural questions.
    - Prepare responses for tricky questions (e.g., salary expectations, reasons for leaving current role).

4. **Create Your Elevator Pitch:**
    - Prepare a concise summary of your experience, skills, and what you bring to the table (60-90 seconds).

5. **Prepare Questions to Ask the Interviewer:**
    - Develop a list of thoughtful questions about the role, company, team, and career development opportunities.

6. **Update Your Documents:**
    - Ensure your CV is up to date and tailored to the role.
    - Print multiple copies of your CV to bring to the interview (if in-person).
    - Bring any additional materials you may need (e.g., portfolio, references).

7. **Check Logistics:**
    - Confirm the date, time, and location (or video call link) of the interview.
    - Plan your travel route if the interview is in person, and aim to arrive 10-15 minutes early.
    - Ensure you have a quiet, distraction-free environment if it's a virtual interview.
    - Test your internet connection, microphone, camera, and any software required for a virtual interview.

8. **Plan Your Outfit:**
    - Choose professional attire that is appropriate for the company's culture (e.g., business formal, business casual).
    - Ensure your outfit is clean, pressed, and ready the night before the interview.

**During the Interview Checklist:**

This checklist will help you remain composed and confident during the interview, whether it's in person or online.

1. **Arrival and First Impressions:**
    - Arrive early or log in to the video call 5-10 minutes ahead of time.
    - Greet everyone with a smile and a firm handshake (if in person).
    - Make eye contact and maintain good posture.
    - Be courteous and respectful to all individuals, including reception staff.

2. **Present Yourself Professionally:**
    - Speak clearly and confidently.
    - Control your body language: sit up straight, use hand gestures where appropriate, and avoid fidgeting.
    - Stay engaged by nodding and maintaining eye contact with the interviewer.

3. **Listen Actively:**
    - Listen carefully to the questions being asked.
    - Take a moment to gather your thoughts before answering complex questions.
    - Ask for clarification if you don't understand a question.

4. **Showcase Your Knowledge and Experience:**
    - Use examples from your previous experience to demonstrate your skills.
    - Refer to your research about the company and role to show that you are well-prepared.
    - Highlight how your values align with the company's mission or culture.

5. **Ask Insightful Questions:**
    - Use the questions you prepared to demonstrate your interest in the company and role.
    - Inquire about next steps in the hiring process.

6. **Closing the Interview:**
    - Reiterate your interest in the role and express enthusiasm about the opportunity.
    - Thank the interviewers for their time and consideration.

**Post-Interview Checklist:**

What you do after the interview is equally important. This checklist will help you follow up professionally and stay organised.

1. **Reflect on Your Performance:**
    - Take a few minutes after the interview to reflect on your performance. What went well? What could you improve next time?
    - Write down any important information shared by the interviewer, such as follow up dates or additional steps.

2. **Send a Thank-You Note:**
    - Send a thank-you email to the interviewer(s) within 24 hours.
    - Mention specific points from the interview to personalise your message.
    - Reaffirm your interest in the position and briefly summarise why you are a great fit.

**Sample Template:** *Dear [Interviewer's Name],*
*Thank you for taking the time to meet with me today. I enjoyed learning more about the [role] and your team.*

*I'm excited about the opportunity to contribute to [specific company/project] and feel that my experience in [relevant skill/experience] would allow me to make a positive impact. Please feel free to reach out if you have any further questions. I look forward to hearing about the next steps.*
*Best regards,*
*[Your Name]*

3. **Follow Up on Next Steps:**
    - If the interviewer provided a timeline for next steps, wait until after that period before following up.
    - If you haven't heard back within a reasonable time frame, send a polite follow up email to express your continued interest.

4. **Stay Organised:**
    - Keep track of the interviews you've completed, the date you followed up, and any responses you received.
    - Continue preparing for other interviews or job applications, even while waiting for a response.

These checklists will guide you through every stage of the interview process, from preparation to follow up. By following these steps, you can present yourself as a polished and well-prepared candidate, significantly improving your chances of success.

**Appendices: Useful Resources for Further Learning**

Mastering interview skills is an ongoing process that can be enhanced through continuous learning. Below is a curated list of books, websites, podcasts, and other resources that can help deepen your understanding of interview techniques, communication, and career development.

**Books:**

1. **"Cracking the Coding Interview" by Gayle Laakmann McDowell**
    - Ideal for those in the tech industry, this book covers 189 programming interview questions and solutions. It also offers advice on how to prepare for technical interviews and how to showcase your skills to potential employers.

2. **"The STAR Interview: How to Tell a Great Story, Nail the Interview, and Land Your Dream Job" by Misha Yurchenko**
    - This book provides a detailed breakdown of the STAR method (Situation, Task, Action, Result), offering numerous examples and tips for handling behavioural interview questions.

3. **"Knock 'em Dead: The Ultimate Job Search Guide" by Martin Yate**
    - This comprehensive guide covers everything from job search strategies and resume writing to networking and interview tips. A great all-rounder for those looking to elevate their interview skills.

4. **"Interviewing: The 101 Best Questions" by James Storey**
    - A handy resource that breaks down some of the best and most frequently asked interview questions, with tips on how to answer them effectively.

5. **"Power Questions: Build Relationships, Win New Business, and Influence Others" by Andrew Sobel and Jerold Panas**
    - While not exclusively focused on job interviews, this book teaches the art of asking insightful questions, which is critical in an interview context.

**Websites:**

1. Glassdoor
    - Provides company reviews, interview experiences, and salary insights directly from employees and candidates. Glassdoor also offers a library of common interview questions by company and industry, which can help you prepare.

2. The Muse
    - Offers expert career advice, including articles on interview preparation, career transitions, and workplace culture. The Muse also has a wealth of resources for job seekers, such as resume tips and insights from hiring managers.

3. LinkedIn Learning
    - Provides a wide range of video tutorials on interview techniques, communication skills, leadership, and other professional development topics. It's an excellent platform for brushing up on both general and industry-specific interview skills.

4. <u>Big Interview</u>
    - A platform specifically designed for job seekers looking to improve their interview skills. It offers video tutorials, mock interviews, and AI-powered feedback to help you practise your responses.

5. <u>Career Contessa</u>
    - A career site tailored for women, offering resources on job searching, interview preparation, career growth, and negotiation. The site also includes webinars and downloadable guides for further learning.

**Podcasts:**

1. **"How to Be Awesome at Your Job"**
    - Host Pete Mockaitis interviews top professionals about workplace productivity, leadership, and career advice. This podcast covers many areas of professional development, including interview preparation.

2. **"The Career Warrior Podcast"**
    - This podcast focuses on job search strategies, resumes, and interview skills. It features industry experts who offer advice on standing out in interviews and securing the job you want.

3. **"HBR IdeaCast"**
    - Hosted by the editors of the *Harvard Business Review*, this podcast covers a wide range of topics, including leadership, communication, and workplace dynamics valuable skills for any professional preparing for interviews.

4. **"The Art of Charm"**
    - This podcast delves into topics like communication, confidence, networking, and professional success, offering practical tips on how to master interpersonal skills essential for making a strong impression in interviews.

**YouTube Channels:**

1. **LinkedIn Learning**
    - The LinkedIn Learning YouTube channel offers free tutorials and insights on a variety of career topics, including interview skills, resume writing, and leadership.

2. **CareerVidz**
    - This channel is focused on providing job interview tips and strategies for all industries, including answers to common interview questions, salary negotiation tips, and advice on professional conduct.

3. **Self Made Millennial**
    - Hosted by career coach Madeline Mann, this channel offers job search and interview preparation advice with a focus on making yourself stand out as a candidate.

4. **The Interview Guys**
    - Jeff and Mike, the hosts, provide in-depth advice on how to answer specific interview questions, giving you scripts, examples, and strategies to succeed in both behavioural and traditional interviews.

**Courses:**

1. **"Interview Mastery: How to Ace Your Job Interview" (Udemy)**
    - A practical, step-by-step guide to mastering interviews, this course covers everything from preparation techniques to how to answer common and difficult questions.

2. **"The Complete Interview Guide" (Coursera)**
    - Available on Coursera, this course provides insights into the entire interview process, including preparation, answering questions effectively, and following up. The course is taught by industry experts and offers practical tools for job seekers.

3. **"Job Interview Skills Training Course" (Skillshare)**
    - This course focuses on developing communication and interpersonal skills to help you make a lasting impression during interviews. It also covers negotiation tactics and follow-up strategies.

**Career Apps:**

1. **Interview Prep App (by PathSource)**
    - Offers hundreds of potential interview questions with explanations on how to answer them. The app provides practice tools to help improve your interview performance.

2. **Glassdoor App**
    - In addition to its website, the Glassdoor app allows you to search for jobs, read company reviews, and view interview questions from other candidates directly from your phone.

3. **Job Interview Coach**
    - This app provides step-by-step coaching, offering tailored tips based on the role and industry you're interviewing for. It also features mock interviews to help you practise.

By exploring these resources, you can deepen your understanding of interview dynamics, improve your confidence, and develop the skills needed to excel in your next interview. Continuous learning is key to refining your approach and staying competitive in the job market.

www.ingramcontent.com/pod-product-compliance
Lightning Source LLC
Chambersburg PA
CBHW052154220526
45471CB00004B/1679